THE CHOICE BEFORE US

Mankind at the Crossroads

THE CHOICE BEFORE US

MANKIND AT THE CROSSROADS

BY

NORMAN THOMAS

AMS PRESS
NEW YORK

Reprinted from the edition of 1934, New York
First AMS EDITION published 1970
Manufactured in the United States of America

International Standard Book Number: 0-404-06389-6

Library of Congress Card Catalog Number: 76-120217

AMS PRESS, INC.
NEW YORK, N.Y. 10003

To the brave men and women, living and dead,
who have made Socialism the hope
of the world

PREFACE

It is a poor book which needs an elaborate preface to explain it. This book must speak for itself and its purpose or speak not at all. But one word of explanation may be in order. The book stands on its own feet. It can be read without reference to anything else I have written. Nevertheless some sections of it are shorter and more summary than would have been the case had I not already written *America's Way Out*. I refer especially to the chapter in which I criticize capitalism and the section in the last chapter which briefly summarizes the immediate economic program of Socialism. Both of these matters as well as the problem of incentive under Socialism and the question of the probable efficiency of socialized industry I have dealt with more fully in my earlier book. That book was written before the depression had revealed its full significance and before the world believed it would have to accept a Nazi victory in Germany with all its sinister implications. It lacked therefore some of that note of urgency which the growth of Fascism must give every socialist argument today.

The Socialist program as I have developed it here goes somewhat beyond my statement of it in the earlier

vii

book in its fuller discussion of confiscation, of the necessity of a capital levy, and of a possible type of government for a Socialist society.

This book has been written at a time of such pressure that it would have been impossible to complete it without the active and eager coöperation of my wife.

NORMAN THOMAS.

January 3rd, 1934.

CONTENTS

CONTENTS

THE CHOICE BEFORE US

Mankind at the Crossroads

CHAPTER I

THIS TROUBLED WORLD

FIFTEEN years ago, almost to the very day, as I write these lines, the Armistice was signed which brought to an end the First World War. The signing of that Armistice was celebrated with such tumultuous joy and expectation as even those with the clearest memories find hard to recapture. The war which had cost the lives of at least thirty million soldiers and civilians, the war which had blotted out the finest and bravest of the whole generation—that war was definitely at an end. The forces pledged to democracy and to the establishment of peace had won. The world was saved.

Today by common consent Europe stands at the brink of war. The situation in the Far East is equally ominous. Men who are honest with themselves must admit that the chief hope of peace in Europe is Germany's lack of heavy arms plus a universal war weariness among the masses which might easily turn new international war into domestic revolt, if not revolution, in any of the great nations. In our own country the chief protection against our possible entry into

1

new world war is nothing nobler than the almost universal conviction that, as the vernacular has it, we were badly stung in the last war.

I was on a trans-continental train when the news came that Hitler had taken Germany out of the League of Nations and out of the Disarmament Conference. Most of my fellow passengers were engaged in discussing the issue most appropriate at the moment; namely, which of the coaches and teams on the Pacific Coast was likely to win the football championship. But in such time as they took from these higher metaphysics they expressed the almost unanimous sentiment that if Europe were foolish enough to get into another war we should know enough to keep out, and that we would not even sell things to warring nations; that is, unless they paid for them in cash!

In other words, after all the talk in the black days of 1914 to '18, that this was a war to end war, after all the bloodshed and the agonies of No Man's Land by men who hoped that by their suffering their sons or younger brothers might be spared such depth of woe, after all the tortuous schemes and easy panaceas which have been proposed in fifteen years of troubled peace, whatever hope there is of avoiding the catastrophe of war, made infinitely more deadly by the onward march of physical science, lies not in the basic ideals or social institutions of men, but simply in their negative fear of war and its possible consequences. International conferences without number, the establishment of a permanent World Court, the much discussed League of Nations, the supposed outlawry of war by the Kellogg-Briand Pact—these and many international conventions and treaties besides, count for nothing, or almost nothing, in the face of the gravest danger that man has ever confronted. The United States and Russia never were included in the League of Nations. Japan, and more recently Germany, have announced their intention of withdrawal from it. The outlawry of war in practice has meant that the nations fight but do not declare war. Japan has taken Manchuria by force from China and has bombarded and occupied Shanghai, with great loss of life, without any declaration of war. Paraguay and Bolivia for almost two years have engaged in sanguinary conflicts over a remote territory in the wilderness without ever declaring war. More money is spent on armament than in June, 1914, and in the world as a whole more men are under arms. Nationalism is certainly more rampant and hate more obviously poisons the relations of nations than it did on the eve of the First World War. The United States, itself somewhat withdrawn from the European maelstrom, has the largest peace-time military budget in its history, except for 1916 when the world was in flames. After years of patient diplomatic work, a badly battered Disarmament Conference was wrecked by Hitler's withdrawal from it. Previously the London Economic Conference, one of the most inclusive world conferences ever held, dissolved in failure.

The more deeply we look into the situation the worse it appears. Fascism, especially of the German sort, more openly, continuously and aggressively glorifies war and inculcates the war spirit than did Kaiser Wilhelm II. at his swashbuckling worst.

The great Soviet Union, nominally the exponent of world-wide solidarity of the workers, and actually in its immediate diplomacy a friend of peace, has nevertheless felt obliged not only to maintain a great system of compulsory service but to militarize education to an almost unprecedented degree. The Fascist countries themselves have not gone farther. No wonder that that best seller, that amazing collection of war pictures with captions by Laurence Stallings, is entitled "The *First* World War."

If that First World War proved anything, it proved the inadequacy at this stage of man's development in an interdependent world of the religion of nationalism with its claims of absolute national sovereignty. We have tried and tried in vain, as the War of 1914 to '18 abundantly proved, to organize our common affairs on the basis of the theoretical equality of nations of very different size and strength, and the actual dominance of mankind by several imperial systems. But nevertheless nothing is plainer than that nationalism has been intensified since the First World War, and that not merely in Fascist states. In our economic life, there has been a curious and very strong revival of the doctrine of the desirability of national self-sufficiency, a revival which reminds one not a little of the mercantilism of the 17th and 18th centuries which led to so many wars, including the American Revolution—a neo-mercantilism which is now loudly proclaimed among highbrows who talk of "autarchy" and lowbrows who shout the familiar slogan: "Buy American," "Buy British," "Buy Japanese." This revival of nationalism is, at least in part, a symptom of the breakdown of the economic order which in the last decade went in for a kind of gamblers' internationalism, a cosmopolitanism of speculation which was the reverse of any true internationalism. In the hour of collapse it has proved easier to make the average American investor, big or little, resent the system under which he bought Peruvian or German bonds than the system under which he bought stocks in Samuel Insull's elaborate structure of holding companies. Yet basically the system was the same, and the collapse of foreign investments was not greater than the collapse of some of the most favored of American securities. By no possible logic can citizens of any nation blame world-wide depression solely on the machinations of shrewd and wicked foreigners. The devastation of economic collapse has been too universal for so easy an explanation.

Poverty and insecurity are, alas, old stories for men.

It remained for this generation, and particularly for this generation of Americans, to invent a new and most bitter type of poverty. Pearl Buck's moving description of famine in a Chinese village is the kind of thing which with minor changes could have been written about agricultural villages over and over again in almost all parts of the world ever since the dim dawn of history. It remained for us to invent "bread lines knee-deep in wheat." Other generations have been poor because they could not produce enough. We are told that we are poor because we have produced too much. For thousands of years man had to accept the inevitability of scarcity. Society would have had the poor always with it, no matter how just and kind might have been its institutions, for the simple reason that man had not learned to harness the powers of nature to help him wrest an abundant living from the earth. It was on the basis of inevitable scarcity that the Greek philosophers tried to justify chattel slavery. Today, as everybody admits, the machine is our slave. We depend not upon the energy of men but upon the energy of electricity to give us at once abundance and leisure. And still in a nation like our own, blessed by every gift man's skill and nature's abundance can bestow, millions of children go hungry. Their fathers vainly seek work that does not exist. They and their families are crowded together in shacks and slums and hovels while the builders of skyscrapers are idle. No satirist ever penned such an indictment of a cruel and lunatic order of society as was written by the author of the Agricultural Adjustment Act in America who saw no way to restore a partial prosperity to farmers except to produce an artificial scarcity by paying agricultural producers from the proceeds of a tax on consumers to destroy the abundance of foodstuffs which men had struggled thousands upon thousands of years to be able to create. And this, be it remembered, in the midst of a cold and hungry world. The more sincerely one believes that such legislation was an emergency necessity the more terrible is the indictment of the civilization which brought it about.

It is not surprising under these circumstances that almost every nation seethes with unrest. It is surprising that men have been so patient. Perhaps the reason is that in the complexities of modern life men instinctively feel that it is not enough to destroy in the fury of resentment, and they do not yet know how to build. Yet that reason can scarcely explain the fact that when Germany reached the point of action her Fascist revolution, beneath its emotional and pseudo-radical dressing, was still essentially capitalist in nature.

It would be unfair to set down this description of our troubled world without recording the fact that by the last quarter of 1933 there has been a slight economic recovery in several countries, notably England and Canada, without the New Deal, and in America considerable recovery as compared with the depth of depression in March, 1933, to the accompaniment of the much discussed New Deal. There was in the United States after the inauguration of President Roosevelt something of an outbreak of health and energy in sharp contrast to the lethargic drift to destruction which marked the Winter of 1932 and '33. As the year drew toward its close this new optimism was decidedly checked as America set about to face the third phase of the depression to which no end was in sight.

To the believer in a new and infinitely nobler order than Fascism there was by the end of the year some hope to be found in the elections in Great Britain, Norway, Switzerland, and elsewhere. They seemed to show that after the debacle of Socialism in Germany under Fascist attack the people were turning again to the principles of Socialism. Russia, which had had an unusually dark Winter in spite of a high degree of success in its five-year plan in industry because of the great difficulties in agriculture under the new scheme of things, was, by the Autumn of 1933, again in a stronger position. A good crop had saved the situation internally and the skill of Soviet diplomacy and the weakness of its enemies had lessened the fear of European or American attack on Russia. American recognition of Russia, fifteen years too long delayed, was a distinct contribution to peace and perhaps prosperity. The troubled world is not without hopeful signs. We are not condemned to fatalistic despair.

Yet there is no denying that the average man in 1933, who has escaped the fanatic hopes of extreme Hitlerite Fascism or possibly of extreme Communism, looked about his world with anxious bewilderment and many forebodings. Many of the things which once he had accepted, at least theoretically, much as he accepted the rising and the setting of the sun, were no longer to be acknowledged by him as among the eternal verities. His religion, if he had kept it, did not begin to mean to him what it had meant to his fathers. Science, which in the first decade of the twentieth century had been associated in his mind and his elder brother's with rational illumination and assured material progress, had become more bewilderingly metaphysical to him than religion itself. In its application to material things it had brought not progress but unemployment, economic insecurity, and the possibility of something like a collective act of suicide in the event of a new war. Democracy, for which he fought or thought he fought in 1917, had been rejected in nation after nation as no blessing. Peace, the average man still craved, but he could scarcely save himself from the repercussions of the extraordinary propaganda, first of a Mussolini and then of a Hitler, to the effect that peace itself is essentially ignoble. Tolerance too, that virtue which was so often praised and so uncertainly and sporadically practiced, had to fight new battles for its place among the social values. The revival of a more than medieval intolerance, symbolized in its extreme form by the lurid flames which went up from Hitler's bonfire of books in Germany, is an outstanding phenomenon to be reckoned with in every program. The half-gods have all but gone, the gods have not arrived.

Yet the march of events does not wait for us to find new gods for old. In the midst of our perplexities we are being rapidly swept onward to action which may determine the fate of generations. We shall be worse than cowards if we sit supinely by. We are not destined either to salvation or destruction regardless of what we may do ourselves. Hence the extraordinary importance for us, especially here in America, to whom in all probability there is a degree of respite from the buffetings of fate not granted to all our European brethren, to explore the situation; to see what choices are possible and how these choices may be made effective.

CHAPTER II

THE BREAK-UP OF THE OLD ORDER

WHATEVER chance there is of our being able to deal competently with the problems of our troubled world depends on a correct diagnosis of the cause of our ills. Without this no general eulogy of planning in general or a particular plan in detail will be of much avail. Much of our loose thinking and looser acting is due to our utter failure to decide the elementary questions: What is wrong with us and where do we want to go, forward to something, or back to something? Ever since the Great War a large section of public opinion, especially here in America, has been talking about returning to something or recovering something. The slogan of one of the most inept and corrupt administrations in American history was "the return to normalcy." The slogan of the boldest of recent administrations is "recovery," and a small-sized economic revolution is being attempted under the guise of a National Recovery Act.

The first condition of a desirable revolution is that we should recognize that we are not recovering something but gaining something. True prosperity is what great masses of human beings have never had. They may win

11

it, they cannot recover it. Yet the fact that, however mistakenly, they continually talk of returning to something or recovering something is proof that our economic system must have functioned better than it does today. With all its crimes and wastes upon its head the older capitalism did work, and what is more it continued to work after the time which many Socialists and other radicals set for its doom. It worked so well that unconsciously many men who still professed a revolutionary faith were not really concerned in wrestling with the difficult problem of creating a new social order but rather with ameliorating the worst abuses of the old and hastening a process of evolution within it. Fired by a natural, appropriate, and, indeed, inevitable, desire which each generation must feel to make life as tolerable for itself as it can, working-class leaders set themselves to the task of getting better hours and working conditions and more security. They permitted the maldistributions of capitalism to continue, and set out to readjust them, after a fashion, by heavy income and inheritance taxes on the one hand and social insurance on the other. They made real progress as anyone can see who will contrast the condition of the workers immediately after the Napoleonic Wars and just before the World War. No small part of the present political bewilderment has come because that progress has ended. In one nation after another it has become more difficult for the capitalist, or more accurately for the capitalist-nationalist, system to carry on and to continue to provide a little more for the workers. In Great Britain for many years the alternative to revolt, even the conservatives tacitly agreed, was rising allowances for unemployment relief. The time came when "to save the nation" the "doles" were cut. The immediate demands of the earlier Fascism in Italy were in many respects radical. Mussolini avowedly intended to promote the national well-being which meant inevitably the well-being of workers. Yet in 1933 there were more unemployed in Italy and real wages were lower than before the famous march on Rome itself. It remains to be seen whether in America—infinitely the most prosperous and fortunately situated of capitalist countries—it will be possible under the New Deal to stabilize capital and out of the surplus take enough care of workers, employed and unemployed, to keep them quiet. Yet for years the old *laissez-faire* system which threw these workers on their own resources managed somehow to keep them quiet because, averaging one year with another, it managed to feed and clothe them rather better than they had been fed and clothed before.

What happened to the system thus to slow it up? Many voices suggest an answer, and most of the answers have some element of truth. One obvious factor in the American situation is that our population, due to the closing of the doors of immigration and a drop in the birth rate, is fast becoming stationary. Hence the mere subsistence needs of an increasing population do not almost automatically absorb the goods our ever-improving machinery can turn out. We have to plan for better houses and more consumption goods for the population we have, and that planning has not been forthcoming. But population is only one factor in the problem. No one in his senses believes that if our population were increasing as fast as Russia's we should then be prosperous without more ado. What, then, do the experts tell us?

We suffer, we are told, from the aftermath of the war and its destruction. We are victims, Sir Arthur Salter and others have warned us, of a particularly virulent form of economic nationalism. On the contrary, affirm certain advocates of "autarchy," we are victims of our failure to build a self-sufficient national economy. Even more numerous and probably more persuasive is the tribe of those who tell us that the trouble is with our system of money and credit. These prophets range all the way from John Maynard Keynes to Coin Harvey —and the range is vast! They advocate everything from Major Douglas's Social Dividend to old-fashioned fiat money. Great as are the differences between them, they have one fault in common; namely, their resolute refusal to see that our system of money, banking, and credit is an integral part of the profit system, and that to rationalize it or socialize it leaving the rest of the system untouched would be a social and psychological miracle and one that could scarcely achieve its desired end. Money is not real wealth, though to our hurt we often confuse it with real wealth. It exists to facilitate the complicated business of exchange. Without money and under barter the machine age would have been impossible. Society suffers worse by using a standard of exchange which fluctuates on its own account as much as the dollar has fluctuated since 1913 as it would were it to use a fluctuating yard or pound. Unquestionably the interdependent and competing monetary systems which some sixty nations have set up have been an immense factor in the breakdown of our system. They have not been the sole or even primary cause of that breakdown.

To use an American illustration, President Roosevelt under his powers of inflation might use clam shells like the Indians for money or print paper like the French and even the Germans during their inflation. At the end of the orgy, if nothing in the meantime had been done directly to change the conditions and terms of the ownership of real wealth, the House of Morgan or its equivalent would be sitting at the top of the heap. If one class of absentee owners was wiped out, another, and perhaps a worse one, would take its place.

The real trouble with our system is at once simpler and deeper than the money reformers will admit. It lies in its basic ideals and institutions. The Marxian prediction of the collapse of capitalism by forces inherent in it was longer postponed than some of its believers had anticipated, but it is being astonishingly fulfilled before our eyes. Capitalism, at any rate the *laissez-faire* capitalism or individualism which its supporters like Adam Smith and Ricardo, and its critics like Marx, regarded as the true and original capitalism, has broken down because its own development destroyed the conditions which gave it whatever justification it had. Simon-pure *laissez-faire* capitalism never existed anywhere unless it was in the pages of textbooks. Nevertheless something like it did exist and worked in a way roughly corresponding to that which the textbook writers described. That way was simplicity itself—at least in theory. There was a being known as economic man who for the purposes of making his own living could be stripped of his loves and hates and prejudices. He knew, or it was his own fault if he didn't know, his own economic gain. He always sought monetary advantage. If he was enterprising he developed his own business. He was in the French phrase the *entrepreneur*. He worked for profit, that is for the difference that his shrewdness and good fortune realized between the cost of what he produced and the selling price.[1] This desire for profit was, as various economic writers have pointed out, the

[1] Will the reader please note the sense in which the word *profit* is used in this sentence and in this book? Occasionally it is used to stand for all the rewards of ownership, profit, rent, and interest. It is never used for the rewards of work. When Socialists talk of abolishing property they do not mean to abolish remuneration for work— as otherwise intelligent people often assume!

steam in the engine. The price system was its governor. Competition or the automatic working of markets brought it to pass without any social planning that the maximum possible advantage for producer and consumer was attained. The intelligent man went where profit was to be found and was warned by a falling off of profits to change the amount or direction of his activity for his own good and for society's.

Of course I have oversimplified the picture as it appeared even to the most devout economists of the Manchester school. They knew before Henry George the complications in their system which the vested rights of landowners created. Most of them were under no illusions concerning the lot of the wage workers. Indeed, it was Ricardo, one of the earlier of them, who formulated the "iron" law of wages which in actual fact proved even under capitalism more elastic than in his theory. England for almost a century accepted free trade, or a near approach to it, not because it was consistent with the .logic of the older economics, but because free trade suited the national interest of a country which wanted to exchange its manufactured goods for raw materials.

But although the *laissez-faire* economics never existed in any pure form it is true that economic individualism worked, especially in a new country like America where first of all unoccupied land and later an unusual number of prizes in the grab bag of life absorbed the energies of the economically energetic. The atmosphere of this individualistic capitalism was friendly to invention and to change. Whether by historical accident or by some intrinsic harmony, the age of machinery began at an early period in the development of capitalism and walked—or ran—hand in hand with that development. So great was the productive power of machinery and the mechanical energy which was applied to it that in spite of all its wastes, its regularly recurring crises, and its ruthless cruelty there was an era of increasing abundance. The exploited were inclined to accept the situation partly because they did share, however meagerly and precariously, in this increasing abundance during the nineteenth and early twentieth century, and partly because they saw some reasonable sanction in a system where the strong or shrewd man took by his own power and kept by his own skill or cunning that which he had taken. The early captain of industry deserved the title. He had to give personal attention to guiding the affairs of the partnership or company in which he was interested. If he was an absentee owner at least he was not an absentee owner in the peculiarly irresponsible sense which later developments in capital made possible. By his savings he did help to provide new capital for new enterprises. The world in which these earlier capitalists ruled could be painted in dark colors. Their society was a predatory society. It was not so fantastic as it later became. The failure of the

Victorian Age to conquer poverty and insecurity was
less terrible because its mechanical capacity was less
well-developed.

This is the situation which, as Marx foresaw, the
march of capitalism inexorably changed. Out of competition inevitably grew consolidation. The invention
of stock companies facilitated an ever-expanding
divorce between ownership and responsibility. The
greater was the expansion of machinery, the more specialized became different forms of human labor, the less
self-sufficient was any individual or any community.
While conservative and radical economists still debate
how extensive was the diffusion of ownership in the last
decade, no honest economist can deny the immense concentration of control which sprang up under our big
corporations, holding companies and the like. Indeed
the more diffused was the ownership the smaller was
the block of ownership at the center which might determine control.

During this process the very nature of the concept
property has been profoundly changed. Professor
Douglas Laing has pointed out that, whereas William
Shakespeare when he made his will was concerned with
such tangible things as, "my second best bed," John
Pierpont Morgan was primarily concerned with those
intangibles which our age, not without irony, calls
securities. It was the ownership of these bonds and
shares of stock which made him master over the lives of

men. The empire of power which he created for himself and his successors was not the result of his inventions, of his technical skill, or of his actual management of any industry. It had as one of its early roots the speculative purchase of inferior arms, condemned for army use, from the Federal Government during the Civil War, which arms, at a time of crisis, he later sold to the same government at an enormous profit. As the years went on his manipulation of stocks and bonds was on a far grander and economically more significant scale than this early adventure in the profits of patriotism, but it was still essentially manipulation. A capitalism which began by giving rewards to frugality, enterprise, and shrewd investment, ended by giving its great prizes to the lucky gamblers. With few exceptions the possessors of great fortunes in America in recent times have been manipulators, men who knew how to take advantage of a piece of good fortune which put them in on the ground floor of things, or of some gambler's hunch with regard to future developments. Consider Mellon's millions! The second, third, and fourth generations from the pioneer millionaires have been able to hang on by the device of trust funds and hired lawyers even after they lost any remarkable gambler's skill. The initiative, which capitalism boasted was furthered by its system of magnificent material reward, has from generation to generation been sadly impaired by the fact that the so-called rights of inheritance made initiative unnecessary. By and large, if one were to draw up a list of great fortunes in America and then try to answer the question, "What have their possessors done to deserve such wealth?" the adequate reply would be, "They have done us."

While capitalism still preached the absolute necessity of the profit incentive, it became more and more dependent in practice on the incentive of the scientifically trained expert, on the restless curiosity which has inspired our age with zeal for finding out some new thing. It hired its brains on the market. With the growth of great consolidations the initiative of the engineer became a hundred times more important than the initiative of the *entrepreneur*. Before Herbert Hoover left office the two hundred largest business corporations, which controlled 50 per cent of our business wealth and were controlled legally by less than two thousand directors, were actually dependent for the conduct of vast enterprises upon the managers, engineers, and skilled workers whom they hired. Profit was an incentive for stock market gambling, so far as the average individual was concerned, rather than for the actual investment of labor with hand or brain. One can imagine nothing more ludicrous—or disastrous—than the spectacle of the stockholders and directors of the United States Steel or the A. T. and T. actually carrying on for a week the enterprises they own.

It was this course of development which steadily

undermined the ethical and intellectual sanctions of the older capitalism. Meanwhile, as we have seen earlier in this chapter, the post-war period, after an orgy of false prosperity within the United States, undermined the pragmatic defense of capitalism, namely that it worked. Of course it never worked well from any ideal point of view. It was always characterized by an atrociously unjust distribution of what was produced. The famous chart prepared by Colonel Leonard Ayres which was once widely circulated in America to prove that "depressions do not last forever" actually showed that since the very beginning of our life as a nation we have never had true prosperity, but were always either coming out of or going into depression. Our record looks like some fever chart that observes a time cycle. As we come down to modern times both its peaks and its depths are intensified. Nevertheless, and the point deserves reiteration, under the union of capitalism with mechanical invention, the rich man's table was so well furnished that even the crumbs often seemed better to the poor than what they or their fathers had had before. Moreover, especially in America, there seemed to be always room at the rich man's table for one more lucky banqueteer.

Today the situation has been changed. Our failure to distribute what we have produced has resulted in damming the channels of production. With all our increase in mechanical skill the actual volume of production has fallen off in recent years. Much of our seeming prosperity in America arose from an overproduction not of goods in general but of capital goods, machinery and factories, which, for example, could produce three or four times as many pairs of shoes as the workers were able to purchase. Under the profit system each new machine went to increase profit, which usually meant discharging workers. All this helped to hasten the day of reckoning. Men had acquired uncanny skill in planning every step in the extraordinary process which ended when the completed automobile ran off the assembly line under its own power. They developed next to no skill at all in planning for balanced production and equable distribution of what was produced. They left them to the profit system, to the automatic workings of markets and the ever-blessed law of supply and demand. That is to say, they thought they left them to the operation of these laws. As a matter of fact by tariffs and subsidies, direct and indirect, by consolidations, by holding companies piled upon holding companies, and a score of other methods they continually interfered with whatever was automatic in the older capitalism, and they substituted no social plan to take its place.

It is an absorbingly interesting question, whether, purely in terms of economics, capitalism has already arrived at the stage where by its inherent inability to plan, and its grotesque maldistribution of the social income, it must continuously produce less and therefore give the workers, whatever palliatives it may introduce, progressively or catastrophically a lower standard of living. This is a position which has recently been cogently stated by Mr. John Strachey in his book, *The Menace of Fascism.* Approaching the subject from a different angle, Mr. Bassett Jones has learnedly argued with the aid of statistics and mathematical formulæ that in any going system the rate of increase of production must bear a one to one relation to the rate of increase of debt, whereas today in America the rate of increase of debt greatly exceeds the rate of increase in production. It is of course possible that the capitalist system might gain a temporary respite by wiping out a large part of that debt either through an orgy of inflation or more scientifically by a capital levy. The former plan would merely create a new middle class and start a new cycle of debt production. The latter might be one of the main dependencies of a society resolved to go Socialist. It would give a capitalist society an extreme case of the jitters.

It is considerations such as these which lead me to doubt whether it is as important as some Communists and Socialists think to fix the exact moment when in terms of pure economics the collapse of capitalism will be inexorably and finally upon us. As a matter of fact, there is still so much wealth in our system and so much productive power, there is still so great a range down which our standard of living might fall before we should come to a mere subsistence level, that it is possible that a capitalism which will use social insurance, even as effectively as it has been used in England, can continue to exist for a considerable time before the workers will prefer to it the uncertainties of overt and violent revolution. On the other hand capitalism might conceivably maintain a standard of existence far above the starvation line, and yet by its injustice, its obvious failure to share the abundance it can produce, and by its general madness, bring about a conscious and revolutionary attempt to change it. In practice we shall deal not with the purely economic effects of capitalism but with them plus their psychological and political consequences and accompaniments. In particular we shall deal with capitalism far more definitely bound to the service of the national state than before the Great War. We shall never have a chance to see whether in terms of capitalist economics Sir Arthur Salter's well-reasoned programs of recovery would or would not have worked for a while. They were wrecked before they were started by the rampant nationalism which set nations to fighting one another with tariffs and with struggles for the possession of gold, even at a time when the guns which they were acquiring in ever-increasing number were stilled in the truce which men call peace.

The conclusion is inescapable that man's worship of his twin gods, the Golden Calf of private profit and the

Moloch of the absolute national state, has cost him
both the will and the intelligence to do what theoretically might have been done to prolong the life of a relatively secure and peaceful capitalism. No one can read
the amazing record of leaders in what we once called
the New Capitalism, a capitalism in which Mr. Walter
Lippmann, writing as recently as 1929, found so much
hope, without being aware that its follies and vices were
inherent in it and not extraneous to it. The striking
fact which stands out in the collapse of Kreuger and of
Insull, and in the revelation of banking practices which
have been spread upon the record, is that it is our outstanding and most respected capitalist leaders who were
involved and who showed their utter incapacity to man-
age their own system. I do not refer now to the moral
aspect of the situation; I do not discuss the plain bad
sportsmanship of a capitalist class, revealed by the Directors of the National City Bank, who lent generously
and without security the money of depositors to their
own officers to buttress their stock manipulations while
they continued to charge low-salaried employees at the
rate of two hundred dollars for each share of stock
after it could be bought on the market for from forty
down to twenty dollars. I do not refer to the morality
or immorality of the elaborate system of bonuses that
has been uncovered, or of the type of speculation which
permitted a famous operator to clean up more than
eleven million dollars on a pool in Sinclair Oil stock

without putting up one cent of real money; or of the conduct of two directors who deliberately sold stock in one of New York's great transportation companies in advance of public knowledge that a dividend would be passed—to their own immense profit. I refer to the extraordinary stupidity of our great business leaders who bought and sold Peruvian and Chilean bonds in blithe disregard of common sense, to say nothing of the reports the wiser of their own experts gave them. To judge from the testimony of members of the House of Morgan, when the storm broke these supermen of business had no incantations against it more powerful than the bleating of the least little lamb whom Wall Street had fleeced. It was a banking house which by reputation combined the best traditions of Plymouth Rock and the Rock of Gibraltar which backed the extraordinary financial racketeering of a Kreuger. When the crash came these gentlemen were, by their own statement, stupider than the farmer who on his first visit to New York bought the Statue of Liberty. He at least saw the statue; they merely believed Kreuger. Mr. Owen D. Young and Mr. Gerard Swope, who probably more nearly than most great capitalists deserve the title of business statesmen, loaned the money of the General Electric Company to prop up Insull's house of cards without such good security as a Morris Plan Bank requires for a twenty-five-dollar loan, and with utter unconcern for the previous rights of the small holders of

Insull's debentures. There is nothing in the record to make one expect from these gentlemen, their associates, or possible successors, more than temporary penitence due to internal sickness and external pressure.

It will be observed that in this analysis of the breakdown of capitalism I have had little to say concerning the effect of the First World War. Doubtless it was great along several different lines. The condition of waging war through four dreadful years was a high degree of collectivization in the management of the economic life of the warring countries. In a moment of supreme emergency the old planlessness of *laissez-faire* capitalism gave way to an economy planned to support a holocaust of destruction. Those economists who optimistically have said that if we succeeded by improvised methods in planning tolerably successfully to carry on a great war we can certainly succeed in carrying on peace, have missed one aspect of war psychology and war economics. There is no problem of overproduction by capitalist standards in time of war. The immense destruction of war acts to create that scarcity with which thousands of years of experience have made men familiar. War planning was not planning to share abundance but to create as large a surplus as possible to support a carnival of ruin beside which earthquake and fire, famine and flood, were as nothing. Moreover the planning in war was made easier because there was the overwhelming motive of fear to lessen the resistance of an owning class to the comparatively moderate restraints put upon it. Everybody knows that these restraints were so moderate that the war actually produced a fresh crop of millionaires. No wonder, then, that in western Europe and in the United States there was a general desire to get away from such methods of social control as had been set up for war purposes and were tainted in popular estimation by their association with war. The popularity of the slogan "the return to Normalcy" did not argue simply a blind and perverse refusal to learn useful economic lessons from the War.

The War and the Peace of Versailles between them led to a capitalism which, despite the tenacity with which it survived, was thrown completely out of balance. As we have already observed, nationalism and hate between nations was increased, not diminished. Economically speaking a large share of American prosperity in the boom period was due to the fact that we lent Europe the money with which she bought from us. We were prosperous while we were increasing our loans of one sort or another to foreign countries. The crash came when it became necessary, under capitalist economics, to collect at least the interest on those loans. Doubtless it was magnified by our unwillingness to take payment in the goods with which in the long run we had to be paid. There is therefore force in the criticism made by the older economists who still hold to doctrines of free trade and easy international exchange.

But not enough force to make the explanation sufficient. Moreover, the realist must insist that the War itself was the product of the capitalist system in alliance with nationalism, and that the peace policies of capitalism were, if not inevitable, at any rate the psychologically appropriate consequences of its own nature and its own follies. Certainly it is too late to repair the damage that was done. The world has definitely seen the end of the type of capitalist progress which roughly speaking lasted up to the War, but which would have come to grief, if not by war, then by economic disaster without war. The probabilities, as we now see in retrospect, would have been for disaster by war, because even if the War of 1914 had been avoided, it would have been expecting too much of men to suppose that forever they could leave all the dynamite of imperialism and militarism lying around and escape the consequences that would follow when some idiot or madman dropped a match. It is our worst danger that fifteen years after the close of that war we have an even greater quantity of worse explosive lying around, and all too probably at least an equal number of idiots and madmen. Another such explosion may be the most likely way of blowing up what remains of our present system. It will not automatically blow us to an earthly paradise. The breakdown of capitalism is one thing; the building of the coöperative commonwealth another.

CHAPTER III

WHAT IS WORTH SAVING?

IT would be clear enough, even if we knew nothing of the recen. history of Soviet Russia, the rise of Fascism in Italy and Germany and the New Deal in America, that the system or chaos we have been describing cannot endure much longer without catastrophe or some profound and significant change. It is equally clear that it is folly to expect it to give rise to a new and better order simply by quiet and almost imperceptible processes of evolution. But before we examine the forces which contend in the shaping of tomorrow's world it may be well to pause for a little to see whether the older capitalist system which has been plunging to its doom has made any contributions to the art of living together worth perpetuating once its power to make progress in meeting our material needs is done.

The capitalism of the nineteenth and early twentieth century was brutal, wasteful, and ugly. Yet it either encouraged or at any rate did not completely stifle certain virtues which until recently men were disposed to admit as desirable without argument. There was about this epoch a certain spaciousness for the individual to express himself, and that not alone in the pursuit of wealth. There was something worth honoring and so far as possible preserving, about the self-reliance not merely of the great, but of humble men in an earlier America. A capitalist epoch saw a genuine growth of the scientific instead of the dogmatic attitude toward truth and with it a degree of tolerance for unorthodox opinion not often matched in the history of a herd-minded humanity. Down to the First World War there was much of genuine respect given to that famous saying of Milton, "Give me liberty to know, to utter, and to argue freely, according to conscience, above all other liberties" which one of the worst of our great newspapers has actually carved in stone upon the magnificent building from which it pours forth distorted news.

I am aware as I write these words how many qualifications I should have to make to them were I recording the years from the French Revolution down to the First World War. Our historians have taught us to see the less lovely side of the "rugged individualism" of the American pioneer. That rugged individualism has become a shadow of its old self in face of the new pressure for conformity produced by the machine age. The growth of monopoly control of jobs and the pressure of new engines of propaganda, like the great newspapers and magazines, the movie and the radio, have tended to bring men to Robot and Babbitt-like conformity. Yet prior to the Great War most of the civilized world would have revolted at the very thought of the conformity which Russia, Italy and now Germany, each in its own way, have established over the minds of their citizens with their approval or at least without their effective opposition.

One of the things which did grow up along with capitalism was a belief in democracy. That belief was often hypocritical, warped, partial, and ill carried out in practice. It went deep. Strongly as we may recoil in retrospect against the slogan, "A War to Make the World Safe for Democracy," we must admit that such a slogan could never have been used had not democracy meant something to masses of people. Nowadays it is the fashion in some quarters under Communist and Fascist influence to decry democracy or what passes for democracy, as peculiarly a capitalist invention.[1] Historically that is not the case. It is true that capitalism with its revolt against the static classification of men which prevailed under feudalism, did demand increased political power for the middle class. In the process it conceded increased political powers to the workers. It is a mistake to think that that power for the workers was a free gift. It was won as a result of the demands of the workers and as a necessary concession to them.

[1] The Communist and Fascist attitudes toward democracy are not the same. The Fascist despises democracy; the Communist believes that his dictatorship is creating conditions which make true democracy possible.

The great leaders of middle-class political movements in the English-speaking world, from Oliver Cromwell down to the writers of the *Federalist,* believed that universal suffrage contained the risk of an attack upon capital. They did not favor it, they opposed it. From the British Reform Laws of 1832 down to the World War every advance of democracy was rightly hailed as an advance for the workers.

In an earlier book I have examined at some length the plight of democracy and the case for democracy. Unquestionably the plight of democracy is worse today than when I wrote because of the triumph of Hitler in Germany. When we consider Fascism and Socialism we shall have to examine that problem more in detail. Here it is only necessary to point out that there was, and still is, a valid ideal in the democratic concept. It is of itself an assertion of the right of the individual, yes, of the individual worker, to be consulted in his own government. It is also the assertion of a belief that orderly processes of change may be facilitated by substituting ballots for bullets. The most impatient critics of the overconservative loyalty of masses of trade unionists in Germany and in Great Britain to an imperfect democracy, ought at least to admit that so tenacious a loyalty must be based on some appreciation of genuine values, not lightly to be brushed aside.

With capitalist democracy went a great amount of civil and religious liberty in our Western world. The long ages of religious persecution, we were persuaded, were definitely and finally over. Religious inquisition seemed to us as unlikely to be revived as cannibalism. The United States never had an established church. France politically was anti-clerical; the established church in Great Britain was tolerated because it was somewhat ornamental and not oppressive. To be sure there were limits to toleration. Force was used against the Mormon Church in the United States to compel it to abandon polygamy which it had supported on religious grounds. Nevertheless it is futile to deny that freedom of conscience in religion, and the right to believe or disbelieve as one wished, seemed to be well established in our world.

It may be objected that the reason for religious tolerance was that men ceased to care as much about religion as they cared about nationalism or the profits of capitalism. Doubtless that was a strong force making for religious toleration. It was by no means the only force in a world which proved its persistent interest in religion by the multitude of creeds which it supported. Moreover, civil liberty was not confined to the field of religion. In the so-called democratic nations there was and still is a great deal of genuine civil liberty. The various diatribes which lovers of liberty have directed against American governmental authorities for their crimes against liberty have usually proceeded on the basis that the excellence of liberty has been accepted and incorporated in our fundamental laws. It is easy enough to prove in this connection that "things aren't what they used to be and never were." In times of emergency and strong passion we Americans never lived up to the Bill of Rights. The Supreme Court whittled our constitutional guarantees almost completely away during the Great War. Toward the Negroes we have practiced and still practice a degree of discrimination and downright brutality which Hitler has not yet taught the Germans to show the Jews. Here we have written a record of shame that admits of little mitigation and no justification.

By the large, Americans have had great liberty of speech and the press. Until the First World War it was amazing the way in which Americans criticized the conduct of the wars in which they were engaged. Except for an occasional interlude there has been a wise and widespread toleration of revolutionary speeches and writing. The Daughters of the one holy revolution whose fame they guard by seeking to enforce birth-control against all other revolutions would be shocked into new panic were any student to print a collection of subversive things said, written, and circulated in America since the inauguration of George Washington as first President, without untoward legal consequences. England, except for the war years, has an even better record in this matter. Among sensible men Hyde Park has been generally acclaimed as the symbol of a policy as wise as it is tolerant.

This liberty of speech, the press, and assembly, has lost ground not only in the war years but in the post-war period. But the apologist for either Communism or Fascism who cites certain notable and shameful abridgments of liberty in America as proof of the utter hypocrisy of our democracy and the complete similarity of conditions here and in Russia, German, or Italy talks nonsense. The very meetings at which he makes his statement, if conditions were reversed, would as a matter of course be suppressed in these countries. In a social order in which tolerance and liberty receive even lip service the victims of gross injustice are far more likely to receive the dignity of significant martyrdom for their cause than under any system of avowed repression. An American who lived through some of the worst years of the terror in Bulgaria and who saw much of similar terror in other Balkan states remarked on the peculiar quality of courage possessed by enemies of the government in power which led them dauntlessly to pursue their way, knowing that for them there would ·be no trial at which they could play Socrates, no chance to live in history by the eloquence of their appeal to their judges or their denunciation of their accusers. Nothing but torture, assassination or execution, and an anonymous grave. Something of the same thing is true in regard to the victims of the Black Shirts in Italy or the Brown Shirts in Germany. It was the indignity of the castor-oil bottle and the loutish cruelty which the Nazis visited upon Jews, Socialists, and Communists which gave to their brutality a sinister effectiveness. Except perhaps for Torgler, Dimitroff and some of their colleagues on trial under the absurd charge that they set the Reichstag Building on fire, Hitler has taken great pains to see to it that the heroes of any resistance to his rule shall be anonymous. Unheralded and unsung, few of them have had a chance to live in history by such speeches as Eugene V. Debs made to his judge and jury; by such an untiring campaign for justice as Tom Mooney has waged from his prison cell; or by such a farewell message as Vanzetti's immortal words:

"You know if it had not been for these things, I might have lived out my life talking on street corners to scorning men. I might have died, unmarked, unknown, a failure. This is our career and our triumph. Never in our full life could we hope to do such work for tolerance, for justice, for man's understanding of man, as we do now by accident. Our words—our lives—our pains—nothing! The taking of our lives—lives of a good shoemaker and a poor fish peddler—all! That last moment belongs to us—that agony is our triumph."

The earlier capitalism at its worst, and Western democracy even at its most hypocritical, was prevented by its own emphasis on the rights of the individual, by its own rejection of any such concept as that of the totalitarian state, from practicing the ruthless and efficient repression which dictators, sure of their historic mission, are now applying in the remaking of their people.

In this period of economic collapse there is a tragic degree of truth in the oft-repeated answer to an inquiry about liberty in a Fascist land, "Liberty, what is your liberty? I can't eat liberty." But it is to fly in the face of history, and to deny what the choicest spirits of great generations have valued more than life itself, to claim that civil liberty and tolerance are not virtues, or to affirm that any bureaucracy, however devoted, can ever be for any long period of time a sufficient substitute for the heretic who has always been the growing point in the development of society. That liberty and tolerance fitted rather more easily into an age of *laissez-faire* and economic individualism than into an age of necessary social control is no reason for assuming that they were by-products of a certain period of economic development, now no longer worth their cost. They will always be necessary if we are to escape from the evil fate of a world where "power corrupts and absolute power corrupts absolutely."

Yesterday's Socialists liked to stress the point that the coöperative commonwealth furnished the necessary basis for any true individualism in a machine age. How could men be free, they asked, when they were dependent for their jobs upon absentee owners of great resources and huge machines? How could they think and think straight, when their whole cultural environment was tainted by the worship of profit, and when the immense machinery of propaganda was always directed in behalf of a class interest to the distortion of ideals and the misrepresentation of truth? Today's Socialists emphasize these same points, but they are rather more aware than their predecessors of the difficulties which attend the propagation of the principle of liberty in a time when social control and the definite purpose of building a new society are of such vital importance.

The war and post-war years have given overwhelming evidence that under certain conditions a strong government can easily bully and cow and cajole the masses. It can keep them in order by a judicious mixture of coercion, or even terror, with bread and circuses. It appeals to mob emotion. In the days when capitalism was young and individualistic, especially in the days when a whole continent was to be won, liberty meant inspiration and encouragement to men in their daily task which it does not seem to mean to men who have to make a living in a complex and crowded civilization where they are utterly dependent upon one another. Unquestionably the average man's bewilderment in the face of national defeat and economic perplexity was a factor in driving Germany to the emotional warmth of a tribal nationalism run by a dictator. These are facts of which all of us who desire to build tomorrow's world must take account, but we shall make a serious mistake if in considering them we decide that there is no fresh strength left in the old virtues of liberty and tolerance. We shall make an equal mistake if we assume that they will be automatically and without effort restored as the coöperative economics of Socialism replace the economics of capitalism. We shall make the greatest mistake of all if we think that man, the individual, will be satisfied to have any state or commonwealth become forever his mind and his conscience—even if, by chance, in such a society he and his fellows are reasonably well fed and entertained.

CHAPTER IV

THE RISE OF FASCISM

HOWEVER complacent Socialists may feel when they consider with what substantial accuracy they foretold the breakdown of the older capitalism, doomed by its own contradictions, they must, if they are candid, admit that they had no distant vision of the Fascist interlude that has come upon the world. To no Socialist theoretician before the War and to few for many years after the War would Mussolini and more especially Hitler have seemed a credible phenomenon in the setting of the modern world. When the incredible happened and Mussolini pulled off a *coup d'etat* which rapidly acquired the significance of a social revolution of a sort, most Socialist observers, like their liberal contemporaries, explained what had happened in terms of the Latin temperament, the comparative backwardness of the Italian industrial development, the immaturity of its democracy, and popular resentment at the failure of Italy to achieve greater material advantage from the War. That Germany would never go Fascist was an article of faith almost up to the eve of the very election when Hitler managed to get a popular majority by more or less democratic methods for the abolition of democracy!

What is this Fascism? How may we explain its rise in the post-War world? How gravely is its extension to be expected—and feared? These are among the outstanding questions for the troubled world.

To begin with, Fascism is not a revolutionary economic order. It is the last stage of capitalism, but of a capitalism upon which Adam Smith would look with horrified wonder. The economics of Fascism in practice, as distinguished from some of its paper programs, is state capitalism; that is, it is capitalism where the power of the state is used to stabilize the maximum amount of private ownership and the operation of the system for the profit of private owners. Gone are the sanctions of the old individualistic capitalism, gone, too, or severely limited under Fascist rule is the personal power of a Krupp, a Stinnes, a Mellon, or a Morgan. The state is supreme and dictatorial, but the landlord, the coupon clipper, and the profit taker still flourish under its ægis.

This brief statement of the economics of Fascism does not altogether jibe with the statements of Fascist leaders in either Italy or Germany before or after taking office. In his most recent important speech—that in which he announced that he would expect the next Italian Parliament to abolish itself in favor of the Guilds—Mussolini took occasion to denounce capitalism about as rhetorically as that renegade Socialist denounced his own former faith. The whole world knows that the German Fascists are Nazis, that is National *Socialists*. Both Hitler and Mussolini recruited their strength largely from among the "little men" or middle-class folk who found their world tumbling to pieces around their heads. So diligently did the Fascists pander to this group that as sound an observer as Scott Nearing sees in Fascism, by reason of its nationalism and its appeal to the "little man" a strong tendency to break up large-scale capitalism and to return, contrary to the genius of the times, to a localized, almost a pre-machine-age, economy. As a matter of fact there has been nothing in the actual development of Fascism, save possibly the decrees in Germany in favor of the peasant proprietors, which shows any material change in the modern tendency to concentration and large-scale units. In Germany the weird hodgepodge which passed for the Nazi program sounded very radical especially in its treatment of "interest slavery." This potential radical-ism precipitated the shift of hundreds of thousands of Communist votes to the Nazi camp in the decisive election, and the entry of a great many young Communists and some Socialists into the Nazi Storm Troops. There was some reason to think that the Nazi dictatorship might be forced decidedly to the left by pressure from within. Instead most of the potential leaders were thrown into jail. No such movement has yet developed.

Pre-Nazi Germany was already highly organized. The state had a considerable share in industry, and there was an elaborate system of cartels, trade associations and the like. Soon after they took power the Nazi High Command put their own men in position to guide or supervise these associations, all the way from the great steamship lines and the metallurgical industry down to the kennel clubs. Not content with the comparatively easy capitulation of the union movement, the dictatorship rounded up the old leaders, mostly Socialist, and consolidated all unions into Nazi organizations. Later the Nazis consolidated the employers and employees of each industry in one allegedly coöperative syndicate. With a flourish of trumpets Hitler created his work army, partly to deal with unemployment, and partly as the nearest approach to universal military service that he could get. Jewish bankers and department-store keepers found that their wealth did not wholly exempt them from an incredibly fanatical and cruel anti-Semitic drive which has loomed large in Nazi policy. All these things have a great social and political importance, but scarcely a corresponding economic importance save as an expression of state capitalism.

In Italy Mussolini, whose political position is secure, has again turned his attention to economic organization. Perhaps he was spurred into new action by President Roosevelt's New Deal, in which he has professed to find the influence of the economics which he introduced into

Italy, perhaps by Italy's unsatisfactory economic position. His recent speeches and actions are chiefly significant because they call attention to the fact that his much-heralded "corporative state" has remained mostly on paper. For many years Mussolini virtually accepted in action *laissez-faire* capitalism with some provisions against lockouts and strikes. Even today Italy has not by any means carried out a scheme for the organization of its economic life through "corporations" which represent the basic Fascist syndicates or Fascist guilds of employers and employees. Labor has been compelled to belong to Fascist unions. The state, which in this case is Mussolini, has from time to time pushed morally and financially some grandiose schemes, especially in the electrical field. As recently as November, 1933, in his speech before the National Corporation, the same in which he denounced both Socialism and Capitalism, Mussolini stated that for the future—not, mind you, for the present—"in industry the corporations will have to assume economic functions, even to taking the place of private initiative and writing *finis* to the capitalist régime as now conceived, creating the best conditions and the most work possible. . . . It is not necessary to confuse private initiative with private ownership. Private property cannot and should not be abolished but in the great industries . . . I regard the *corporazione* [corporations] as the organ which will control." The ex-Socialist has traveled a long road which must be as bewildering to the "little men" of the middle class, from whom largely he recruited his supporters, as to the left-wing Socialists whom he had previously deserted. Private ownership, be it noted, is to continue to exist without the old justification that it was needed to spur initiative. Great industry is to be pushed forward, if Mussolini can do it, on the American or Russian scale, and although the supreme control may be in the state the profits will still go to private owners. The structure of syndicates and guilds or corporations, if and when it functions somewhere else than on paper, will still be under the absolute dictatorship of the Fascist party. Under these circumstances it does not matter much, economically or politically, whether or not Mussolini finally abolishes the Parliament in favor of the National Council of Corporations or some other body. Already his Chamber of Deputies is a body of rubber stamps with scarcely the nuisance value of the New York Board of Aldermen.

It is impossible in this scheme of things to find any serious answer to the essential problem of production for use. The stabilization of capital in Italy, such as it is, the minor concessions to workers and peasants, have meant singularly little to them in economic well-being. Italy has been caught with the rest of the world in depression. Mussolini has neither abolished unemployment nor done as well for the unemployed as non-Fascist England. Real wages are decidedly lower than in the bourgeois democracy of France which Mussolini despises. The trains may run on time but all the Italian worker has gotten out of it is a sense of pride in being Italian. "They call us Italian instead of Dago or Wop," as one of them told a friend of mine.

There is food for thought in the fact that a system which offers to the producing masses nothing more by way of economic advantage than Italian or German Fascism has as yet produced, can continue in such strength. It seems to show that so great is the productive power of modern machinery that a relatively slight stabilization of the system which cures none of its fundamental defects can yet avert for a considerable time complete economic catastrophe or paralysis. It certainly shows that men can be coerced or cajoled into accepting pathetically little in a world which might give them abundance, provided the dictator can give them such emotional satisfactions as come from their personal identification with the glory of their nation and the grandeur of their race.

What is newest and most significant in Fascism, Italian and German alike, is not its economics, which all the multitude of words of all the propagandists cannot make anything but a form of capitalism; rather it is the extent to which it has driven the notion of the sovereignty of the national state exercised under a party dictatorship. Ever since the French Revolution nationalism has been the religion of Western man. It helped to drive him into the hell of 1914 to 1918 and sustained him in it. It remained for Fascism to develop a concept of the totalitarian state which should absorb not only in war but in peace the loyalty, the energy, and the conscience of men. The state became to Fascists a mystic entity, something even more than Hegel's expression of the "general will" and certainly more than the expression of the coercive power of a ruling class which is the rôle assigned to it in Marxian theory. It exists not for the individual but the individual for it. War rather than peace is the highest expression of its grandeur, and in serving it in war a citizen is to find his highest exaltation. All this had its roots in various of the pre-War philosophies and in the tumultuous patriotism which was intensified by the very war which proved the tragic inadequacy of absolute nationalism for organization of an interdependent world. Before Hitler seemed anything but a rather feeble joke Carleton Beals and other writers were able to trace, both for Mussolini's conception of the totalitarian state and for his ideal of violence, a respectable ancestry. It was Hitler's achievement, or rather the Nazi achievement, to accomplish the well-nigh incredible task of developing and carrying into practice a concept of the state worse than Mussolini's. For Hitler, Goering, Goebbels, Rosenberg and their colleagues, in an age when nationalism had outgrown a primitive tribalism and accepted the fact that nations were of mixed blood, set out to restore Germany to an Aryan or Teutonic or Nordic purity of race which has not existed anywhere for centuries. They found their historic justification for this in the fantastic pseudo-science of Gobineau, a Frenchman, and Houston Stewart Chamberlain, an Englishman. They found their principal victims in the Jews. Anti-Semitism, like nationalism, is not new. It remained for the Fascist movement in twentieth-century Germany to carry it to lengths which may have set back the clock of human progress not by generations but by centuries.

It is a serious error, however, to suppose that the evil of Hitler's conception of the state lies primarily in its tribalism and anti-Semitism. It lies rather in the concept of the totalitarian state, which is shared with Italian Fascism. That is, it lies in the notion that in an age when the labor of men of all races and nations gives us not only our culture but our daily bread one nation can sum up all man's loyalties and all his devotions. The Fascist state has crushed all the independent life of labor unions and coöperatives. Out of both Italy and Germany it has driven their finest spirits because they will not give it the quality of allegiance which no creative spirit can give to one of the least worthy of the long line of historical claimants to the rôle of God over the lives and hearts of men. It is true enough that both Mussolini and Hitler have had to tolerate the Roman Catholic Church which they have even tried to use, but clearly they are jealous of it. In

Germany the Nazis have tried to remake the less venerable and less international Protestant Church in their own image. And it is significant that after some initial success they have met with opposition bolder, and so far more successful, than the opposition in labor unions. Liberals throughout the world, and the whole Jewish people, would have been better off if they had not so easily made peace with Italian Fascism because it had "checked Bolshevism" and "made the trains run on time." It ought to have been evident from the beginning that any economic group with culture of its own stood in imminent peril because of the claims of the totalitarian state to absolute conformity. The fact that Italian Fascism was not anti-Semite was primarily due to the fact that there were few Jews in Italy, and that there was no political advantage in turning the political discontent of people from bankers and capitalists in general to Jewish bankers and capitalists in particular. There was no great merit in Mussolini's failure to treat Jews as he treated Socialists, Communists, the Catholic Popular Party, and even Freemasons; no virtue for him that when he crushed all freedom of the press and of discussion his intolerance had none of the peculiar reference to Jews which has written so many black pages in German history and has forced so moving and bitter a testament as Jakob Wassermann's *My Life as German and Jew*. That was an historical accident due to the fact that the few Italian Jews never challenged Fascism or any of its concepts. Yet, in America, certain Jewish editors have nominated Mussolini among those Gentiles who have done most for the Jews or for decent relations with them. And one of the most militant Jewish opponents of German Fascism assured me that he had no quarrel at all with Italian Fascism, not only because Mussolini had saved his people from Bolshevism, but also because he had Jews in his Cabinet! It is this utter failure of the bourgeois leadership of the Jews to understand the philosophy of freedom on which the well-being of the Jewish community depends, whether one regards that community as expressing race, religion, or culture, which strikingly illustrates the inadequacy of the bourgeois liberalism of the nineteenth and early twentieth century, confronted with the passions of a revolutionary epoch. That liberalism rarely gave much more than lip service to freedom in general as opposed to the particular freedom which it sought for one group or class.

How such a movement as Fascism, with its medieval intolerance and more than medieval insistence on conformity, could establish itself in the modern world is of profound concern to all of us. Neither dictatorship nor terror is new in the world. Both of them have been used in the service of Communism in Russia. The ruthlessness and cruelty of Fascism have been equalled, in some cases exceeded, under more old-fashioned dictatorships, like Machado's in Cuba, Pilsudski's in Poland, and the various lords of misrule who curse the Balkans. But Italy and Germany are modern states. In neither of them was the older democracy as firmly established as in England, France, or America. Germany, however, was historically the home and the hope of the Socialist movement. It was a great industrial nation with what was generally regarded as the finest educational system in the world and with a new constitution which was the last word in liberal theory.

To explain the phenomenon of Fascism in either Italy or Germany in terms of radical or national biology or to argue that any nation is inherently immune to it is to use a pseudo-science as false and misleading as Hitler's own. If we are to generalize, we can say only that Fascism is the last stand not only of capitalism, in an economic sense, but of the whole middle-class culture and prestige, both of which had been warped and twisted by the passion and fear dependent on war, a disappointing peace, and economic collapse. This statement cannot stand without qualification and explanation. Fascism both in Italy and Germany in its days of struggle had invaluable financial support from various great industrialists and certain militarists. It was not, until the very end in Germany, the *first* choice of business interests and certainly not of Hindenburg. They finally embraced it or accepted it as preferable to confusion, to aggressive Socialism, or to Communism. The first strength of Fascism as the Fascists themselves insist was with the more vigorous of the middle class, especially young men and women including the young intellectuals, who came to the threshold of life, for which many of them had been well trained, without prospect of a job.

The middle class, which turned the scales in favor of Fascism, was perhaps more truly middle class because of its psychological outlook and aspirations than in a strict economic sense. Both Socialism and Communism have paid a heavy price for their failure to make the mass of white-collar workers and young intellectuals realize that they, too, should have been numbered among the builders of the coöperative commonwealth; that they have far more to gain from a genuine emancipation of the working class than from any precarious place they could find or make for themselves among the *petit bourgeois.*

One cannot read such an account as Professor Salvemini has given of the rise of Fascism in Italy or Calvin Bryce Hoover's admirable study, *Germany Enters the Third Reich,* without marveling at the skill with which Mussolini and Hitler held together such various groups which by no means were united by a common interest. That, rather than any genuinely creative ability, was their strength. They could not have held these forces at all by the kind of capitalism which seemed to Calvin Coolidge and his American con-

temporaries so sound and so well-established and which
our Chamber of Commerce would now restore. Mussolini, long after he had left the Socialist party, supported the workers in taking physical possession of certain great factories. One of his semi-official defenders,
speaking at an important conference in America some
two years ago, expressly declared that it was the essence
of Fascism to have no program except its veneration of
the state, and that if and when Mussolini came to believe that Communist economics would work in Italy
for the glory of Italy he would apply them. Whatever
the elements of confusion or insincerity in the Nazi program, it would give cold shivers to an American Chamber of Commerce. It has not been carried out in any of
its more Socialist or radical aspects, but neither has it
been repealed nor revoked. It is, I think, more significant than is commonly realized, that while capitalism
has shown immense power of survival and adaptation
in its Fascist stage, it has nevertheless been obliged to
surrender a great deal of its own arrogance and initiative. Whatever else the dictatorships of the world are,
they are not the sort which, if applied in his own country, would please Mr. Andrew Mellon, save as the less
of great evils. Even in Japan, where the real power
is in the hands not of a Fascist party, but of a group
of chauvinist militarists, the virtual dictatorship has
recently compelled the enormously wealthy Mitsui
family to make a contribution of 30 million yen for the

aid of the economically distressed. It is notorious that the Conservative party in England has had to accept immensely heavy taxation, by capitalist standards, as the price of survival. It is only in America that, at least until the end of the Hoover Administration, a capitalist class expected to survive without substantial concessions in outward power and prestige and usually in profits. Hitler, with what in retrospect must be regarded as extraordinary skill, managed to make the capitalists of Germany understand that, if he were to be their savior, it would be on terms very different from those they thought they had laid down to von Papen in the days of his short-lived glory.

Moreover Fascism cannot be explained as a simple economic reaction to economic forces. Although both in Italy and Germany its own leaders claim that it was born out of economic collapse, the term is somewhat of an exaggeration. Worse economic conditions in other parts of the world have not produced Fascism. Professor Salvemini makes his case that disorder was lessening and economic conditions improving in Italy before Mussolini made his march on Rome. He may have introduced a certain stability in Italy; the evidence is plain he did not improve basic economic conditions for the workers. Consideration of the relative position of Italy and Germany in a troubled world must go into any explanation of the rise of Fascism. We have already considered how important an element in Fascism, is the

religion of the national state. Italy went into the World
War on a cold and calculating appraisal of national
advantage. It came out on the winning side but without
the glory, the territory, or the economic gain it desired.
It could not easily reabsorb its young soldiers in civil
life. Mussolini put a lot of them in black shirts and
gave to their gangsterism some discipline and a high-
sounding cause. With them, aided financially by certain
big industrialists, and by a great degree of sympathy
inside the army itself, Mussolini won his *coup d'etat.*

In Germany, where national humiliation and discontent were greater than in Italy, Hitler won not by mobilizing discontented soldiers fresh from the War, but by
mobilizing a generation which had not had first-hand
experience in war. His propaganda was longer and
more intricate than Mussolini's, and in the end he won,
not by a *coup d'etat* but by an election in which democracy, under pressure from his Storm Troops, voted its
own death warrant. Authorities may quarrel as to the
precise manner and degree in which German anger at
defeat, at the unjust Peace of Versailles, the preposterous reparations, the occupation of the Ruhr, and
compulsory disarmament in an armed world, operated
for the advancement of Fascism. It is impossible to
believe that without these conditions the German situation would ever have resulted in the growth of Hitler to
a power that Bismarck never had. It is true that before
Hitler came into power some of the worst of the injus-

tices from which Germany suffered under the Peace Treaty had been, or were in the way of being, repaired. It was a prelude to tragedy that to the German people it appeared that the rising tide of Fascism, even before the Nazis got power, compelled the Allies to make concessions on reparations that they had never made to Stresemann or to the Social Democrats. Not often has it been more strikingly proved that in human affairs it matters not only to do the right thing but to do it before it is too late.

Dorothy Thompson in writing and speaking about the Nazi triumph has stressed another factor in it. That is the bewilderment that the average man felt when faced with the economic and political troubles of the times. He could not escape by going out into a new country to stake out for himself a homestead. He could not escape by any personal effort. He wanted security and the gregarious warmth of the crowd more than hazardous pioneering in coöperation. Conceivably he might have found these things in Communism; but Communism was foreign in control, and what he saw and heard of living conditions in Russia did not make him think that he had much to gain by surrender to it. From this point of view the Nazis' triumph was a victory for the crowd mind over the individual and his love of liberty.

In Germany both Socialism and Communism, which had a long head start on Fascism, have a great deal of explaining to do of their own failure to meet the desires of the masses well enough to make the rise of Fascism impossible. They failed in Germany somewhat as they had earlier failed in Italy, and with less excuse, to produce the leaders, the solidarity, and the energy, to achieve victory. They alarmed the middle class without conquering it or making an effective alliance with any section of it. Both in Italy and in Germany Fascism was the road chosen by people who were disturbed by Socialism and Communism and feared the victory of either of them. Manifestly, however, it could not have been merely the weakness of Socialism and Communism which led to Fascist triumph. However anachronistic such a victory seems in a modern interdependent world it was not achieved simply as a result of negative weaknesses of its enemies, but because it did correspond to certain powerful interests, passions, and prejudices to be found among men.

What of the future? There is no answer to this question which does not take into account, on the one hand, the disintegration of capitalism and the capacity of the world to return to barbarism, with the barbarians riding in automobiles and airplanes instead of on horseback, and, on the other hand, of the growth of Socialism and Communism, which we shall later discuss. Scott Nearing still believes in the face of the Fascist record of not checking the growth of big business, that the totalitarian state cannot operate over a large area. This fact combined with the appeal that Fascism has made to the little man will mean in Fascist nations a gradual return, or an attempt to return, to something very like a pre-machine-age economy. He has spent too much time in Germany and Italy for his prophecies to be dismissed as empty, but I see nothing in the course of events to give them weight. Neither do I see much reason for the hope of those who believe that Fascism will soon be transformed from within to a genuine Socialism or Communism, with ultra-nationalistic features which will gradually fade away.

It is possible that Fascist economy like capitalist economy everywhere will break of its own weight and by that fact create a domestic situation favorable to revolution. It is more likely that before that can happen a Fascist dictatorship will plunge its country into new war which indeed may involve all Europe before Fascism has had time to win fresh victories in non-Fascist nations. There is a theory that Fascism, because of its concentration on the domestic life of the nation, may be as peaceful as, or even more peaceful than, the older capitalist imperialism. Again it is a theory not in accord with observable fact. Mussolini is concentrating his attention none too successfully on building up Italy economically, but he has never retracted his earlier references to a grandiose scheme to restore the Roman Empire. He has definite colonial ambitions which are bound to bring him into further clash with the French.

It is a cardinal principle of Nazi philosophy to bring all territories inhabited by the German people into one Reich even though Hitler professes no great interest in colonies. Trotsky has pointed out that Hitler's hope of military power consists in persuading western Europe that Germany rearmed may be a bulwark against Bolshevism. Since, like all militarists, Hitler believes that the best defense is an attack there arises from this source new danger of war. In general the whole spirit of Fascism, as the Nazis have especially emphasized, is military. There is a mystical quality about their eulogy of warlike virtues, and this is reflected in the tone they seek to give to the national life of Germany and the education of its people. No one can go in for this sort of military culture without paying a terrible price.

The spirit of Fascism is contagious among nations. Nor is it any longer as dependent as it was for success on a national inferiority complex. In some form an avowed Fascist nucleus exists in almost every land. In most of them some form of it seems likely because it is the best hope for the prolongation of capitalism. Austria is all too probably its next victim. No nation is altogether immune—certainly not the United States of America. But in the spread of Fascism there is no hope of peace through the agreement of those who share a common belief. By its very nature it must be divisive, not unifying, and make for war, not peace.

Looking to the future there is only one hope that the

optimist has to offer. It is that at least Fascism is preparing a psychology and a technique of collectivism which the coöperative commonwealth may use. To which the pessimist replies: "But it is doing this by identifying collectivism with the servile state. It is preparing men for some such horror of stratified conformity wherein Babbitts and Robots are scientifically bred and trained and placed, as in Aldous Huxley's *Brave New World*," without the internationalism which made that world a world of peace. I am on the side of the pessimist. Fascism is the evilest spawn of capitalism and nationalism, of the acquisitive society and war.

CHAPTER V

SOCIALISM AND COMMUNISM

MAY DAY, 1933, and the weeks immediately there-
after saw both the rival parties of the working class,
Socialist and Communist, at perhaps their lowest ebb
of hope, vigor, and achievement since the Armistice.
In Germany on May Day, Hitler staged in the first flush
of his full power a nationalistic demonstration far sur-
passing anything the Socialists had ever thought of stag-
ing in the historic home of Socialism, when they were
leading a political revolution in the name nominally not
only of democracy but of internationalism. Hitler, on
his nationalistic May Day, was continuing against
Socialists, Communists, and Jews a peculiarly brutal
and ignominious terror. But the strongly organized
forces of the workers, Socialist and Communist alike,
had broken before him almost without resistance. Their
leading spirits were in jail, concentration camps, or
exile. Their most daring workers had been driven to
underground activities. In the country of Lassalle, Bebel,
Liebknecht, Kautsky, and Bernstein, the beneficiary of
the break-up of the old capitalist, nationalist order was
not the international proletariat under the leadership of

any of its various parties but a shrewd, intolerant, half educated, nationalist fanatic and demagogue.

If Germany was the supreme tragedy, the situation in the Spring of 1933 was not encouraging to Socialists or Communists anywhere. There was no serious opposition to the power of Mussolini in Italy. The Socialists of Austria, who had made Vienna a model of what Socialism might do even with the limited powers of one municipality, were ground under the heel of the little Chancellor Dollfuss, who was only a few degrees less bad than the German Fascists whom he fought in the name of an Austian nationalism patronized by Mussolini. Hungary lay quiet under the White Terror which years ago had succeeded the Red. Poland, without the concessions to the masses supplied by Fascism, was still governed by the half-mad dictator Pilsudski who long before had lost whatever Socialism he had. In Europe, capitalist dictators or parties still held sway in states where, after the war, Socialist triumphs had seemed inevitable, and this in spite of the fact that it was obvious that under their rule their nations drifted toward catastrophe. The outstanding exception was Spain which had achieved a peaceful revolution politically and had embarked upon a series of profoundly significant social changes. Yet even in Spain, by May Day, 1933, there were evidences of the conservative and clerical reaction which was later to threaten the best results of the revolution. In England the Labor party was recovering its morale after a serious defeat brought about not so much by the defection of Ramsay Mac-Donald, which defection was a blessing in disguise, but by the failure of the party, which had long held on to office at the price of real power to do anything worth while in Socialist construction.

In America President Roosevelt's shrewdness and vigor had somewhat checked the disintegration of capitalism and certainly prevented a long chapter of riot and confusion. But it was not an alternative to a Socialist or Communist revolution because the working classes, despite the worst depression in American history, were obviously not prepared or preparing for that on any effective scale. Election figures are not the only signs of popular feeling but they are a sign, and a sign of importance. In November, 1932, the total vote of all minority parties had been only 1,232,824. Even if one doubles this figure in a generous attempt to restore votes unquestionably stolen from, or not counted for, the minority parties, the total is not encouraging.

Such facts and figures as those which I have just been recording are usually cited to prove the breakdown of social democracy and the parliamentary method. But they are not more encouraging for Communism. What progress Communism was making May Day, 1933, was mostly in China. It was precisely in those countries where capitalism seemed most obviously over-ripe that Communism was gaining most slowly. It was still an almost insignificant force in England and the United States. It was not very powerful in France. It had lost to Hitler in Germany. It was losing ground in Czecho-Slovakia. Even in Communist Russia on May Day progress seemed to be marking time. Russia had achieved wonders under the Five-Year Plan in industrial organization, but the ruthless attempt to force agricultural collectivism by a kind of factory system on the farms had not only created great discontent—that, in the Russian scheme of things, might have been crushed by wholesale removals of populations—but it had failed to provide the country with adequate food. There is significant testimony on this point from Professor Calvin Bryce Hoover, who, as author of *The Economic Life of Soviet Russia,* had proved anything but an unfriendly observer. In his new book, *Germany Enters the Third Reich,* Mr. Hoover writes: "During the latter part of February the writer had revisited Soviet Russia for a few days after an absence of some three years. In Russia there was famine, an increased terror and the failure to realize the economic expectations of the spring of 1930. The writer had returned to Germany with the feeling that if the National Socialist régime was the alternative to Bolshevism then much could be forgiven it. If a curtailment of individual liberty under a dictatorship were the price which had to be paid to avoid the unlimited terror which held sway in Russia, then the price seemed worth paying." Mr. Hoover goes on to explain that the "conditions of terror in Russia were rapidly being duplicated in Germany." Here we are concerned with what he says about Russia, a statement borne out by the testimony of most observers. Some appreciation of the fact had reached the minds of the American masses. In the depth of depression in the Winter and early Spring of 1933, speaking before working-class audiences in many parts of the United States, I heard fewer references to Russian success than I had been hearing a year or so before.

A study of developments in Germany under the Fascist dictatorship, and in Russia under the Communist, is all to the advantage of Russia. The concept of the totalitarian state is infinitely more dangerous to the future than the acceptance of a temporary dictatorship for a transitional period. There are in the latter corrective elements, a conscious desire for a new social order freed from the exploitation of a profit-making class, and an economic program, which are wholly lacking in Fascism. The tendency of life in Russia is up, and not down, which is more than can be said for Germany. Developments since the May Day of which I have been speaking have been encouraging in Russia. The government successfully, if ruthlessly, crushed the active or passive revolt of the peasants in the Ukraine. Some errors in the application of the agricultural policy were corrected. The Red Army was put to work at sowing and harvesting. Nature was kind; Russia had a good crop. Her diplomacy had been both pacific and successful. Belated recognition by the United States is of value to both countries and probably to the peace of the world. Stalin's policy of concentrating everything on constructive building in Russia is bearing fruit. Inevitably it makes for a certain degree of nationalism in practice, but as yet it is not an imperialist nationalism. Russia has been patient, until very recently extraordinarily patient, in dealing with Japan and Manchuria. To Germany, despite the number of Communists in concentration camps in Germany, Russia has made no more protest than the United States, and her influence has held back the Third International from advising the workers to boycott Germany. What will be the psychological tendency of all this on the future of a proletarian internationalism remains to be seen. Unquestionably Russian stock is rising again and with it the repute of Communism. The latter might rise higher and faster were it not for the long-range dictatorial control exercised from Moscow, not technically from the Russian Government, but from the Headquarters of the Third International, dominated by Russians and by Russian interest. There has not been even a full-fledged Congress of the Third International to check Russian control for seven years.

It was not only Russian Communist skies which were brighter in November than they had been in May. In spite of a disappointing conference of the Second International held in Paris during the Summer of 1933, various Socialist parties, with the important exception of Spain, were able to show encouraging gains in electoral favor by the end of the year. Municipal elections in Switzerland and Great Britain, parliamentary elections in Norway, and by-elections in Great Britain resulted in victories. In its annual conference, the British Labor party, which the year previously had repudiated the policy of holding onto office at the price of real power, took the advance step of declaring in favor of no budgetary support for war and a general strike against war. In Europe, in general, outside of Russia the reaction to Fascism strengthened democratic Socialism rather than dictatorial Communism. Yet with all these encouragements it would be folly to try to explain away the setback which both Socialism and Communism received from Hitler's triumph. It is equal or worse folly for Socialists or Communists to try to sidestep examination of the situation by blaming each other for the German debacle.

It would take an expert knowledge of the German situation during these last sixteen years to which I do not lay claim to pass anything like a final judgment on the record of either Socialists or Communists. Yet the effort to reach some general conclusion is indispensable as a guide to any policy for furthering Socialism and fighting Fascism.

In so far as our judgments imply criticism we must

be humble. America as a whole was partner to the War, the Peace, and the post-War madness which prepared the way for Hitler. The men we are criticizing have paid dearly for their mistakes, some of them with their lives and others in imprisonment and exile. There is now an underground activity among the rank and file of the workers in Germany shrewdly and heroically carried on which is bound to bear fruit. But to record these facts still leaves the problem of Socialist failure to be considered.

One of the least satisfactory judgments on Germany is the blanket and unqualied statement, "Democracy failed in Germany as the tool of Socialism, dictatorship succeeded in Russia as the tool of Communism, therefore Socialists everywhere must abandon democracy for dictatorship." Such a statement does not even try to find out what kind of democracy failed in Germany or why, what kind of dictatorship succeeded in Russia, and under what conditions. It ignores the fact that the dictatorship which succeeded in Germany was Fascist and not Communist.

To my mind it seems clear that a large part of the reason for the failure of the German Social Democracy goes back to the War itself. The majority, the big majority, of German Social Democrats supported the War. They supported it to the end, although toward the end they did work harder than some of their critics now will admit for a negotiated and reasonable peace.

However, the leaders were so absorbed in war and a negotiated peace that they had no plans for revolution and took reluctant advantage of the revolutionary opportunity which the defeat of the German Army after four years of struggle against great odds had bestowed upon them. They had some ideas about a political revolution from the Empire to a democracy, but they had fewer ideas about Socialist construction and they lived for months in well-founded terror of occupation of Berlin by the Allied Army if they made a genuine social revolution. They doubted, with some reason, how far the German people were ready for that revolution. They believed it would emerge in the process of time by democratic processes, and the insurrectionary Communism of a German minority which miscalculated times and seasons not only put upon the German Social Democratic temporary goverment the onus of having to put down insurrection, which Noske did all too ruthlessly, but forced it to a more conservative position. It became easier than ever to put democracy, and a rather mechanical democracy at that, ahead of Socialism.

In retrospect it seems astonishing what obvious things the German Social Democratic leaders overlooked. They failed to use the months of their real power after the Armistice for effective propaganda and education. They could have learned much if they could have foreseen some of Hitler's propaganda methods. They left reactionary judges in office, and high civil service officials in positions where they could sabotage Socialist attempts. They deserved credit for trying to make a constitution which should be the last word in enlightened and progressive democracy. They did not sufficiently consider how well it would be adapted to the turmoil of post-War years. When the constitution was adopted, the German Social Democracy was content to become a constitutional party under it. In spite of the continual cry of Hitler, echoed from a different point of view by the Communists, that it was German Socialist government which through fourteen years ruined Germany, that country after the first months of the Republic lived either under coalition government or under government in which there were no Socialists at all. Socialists were in a minority even in the constitutional convention. They shared in coalition governments only sixty-four months in fourteen years. From 1930 on the Socialist party contented itself with becoming a sort of balance of power and choosing the lesser of two evils. It did not develop vigorous constructive plans of its own or vigorous leadership. It took Hindenburg because it feared Hitler, and it got both. The final revelation of its weakness was to be found in the fact that before Hitler came to power von Papen was able to remove the Socialist government of Prussia by decree, backed by no other force than a handful of policemen! It seems fairly clear that, if the Social Democratic party had had any vigorous leadership and if its leader had not been, with some reason, afraid of what Communists might do, the workers would have responded to a general strike as once before they had responded to the general strike which defeated Kapp's Monarchist Putsch. Apparently the German Social Democratic leaders were equally afraid of a general strike whether they should win or lose.

Yet it would be less than accurate to attribute the German failure entirely to leaders. The frequent German elections showed that the great majority of the workers went along with moderate policies. The German Trade Union leaders were a brake rather than a spur to the party. The more skilled and better organized of the German workers saw nothing in Russia which they envied for themselves. Under the elaborate cartels and codes which labor enjoyed in the pre-Nazi régime, the workers became insensibly industry- rather than class-conscious. Their representatives, who had rights not yet granted to American workers under our codes, met with the employers. Together coal miners and the heads of the coal industry considered the plight of the industry, and its need of higher prices. More and more labor was content to let the industry claim higher prices no matter what happened to the mass of workers as consumers, provided that with those prices went slightly increased wages. Two of the best informed of the Social Democratic refugees whom I have met, independently of each other, have placed this breakdown of any real solidarity of workers under the influence of this system of industrial organization high among the reasons why German labor was not more effective. All of this constitutes a convincing indictment of the folly of workers who put their trust in *capitalist* democracy and its automatic working, or in their chance of driving to power without struggle through a process of nose counting in endless elections.

But German Social Democracy had real virtues for which the world now gives it too little appreciation. It had a passionate love of the peace of the nation for which it was willing to sacrifice much. Its essential tolerance (after the Noske period) was a characteristic without which there will never be a happy world. What in the retrospect it seems to have lacked was vigorous leadership and aggressive action on a well-thought-out plan. These are equally necessary both for a democracy and for a dictatorship. More and more in practice the Social Democratic policy was negative. It opposed the Fascists, it opposed the Communists, it opposed the increasingly dictatorial policy of the cabinets pushed into office by a coalition of capitalist parties. It did not go out to the country with a ringing and positive challenge. It was loyal in professed devotion to the Marxian word but failed in the Marxian deed. (By the way, it must be remembered that Marx himself had had little enough to say about the deed, that is about the constructive business of building the coöperative commonwealth.

Perhaps, as H. G. Wells has frequently argued, that has been one trouble with Socialist construction.)

But the followers of Lenin, who certainly had a program of action, did not cover themselves with glory in Germany. Their leadership was fearfully cramped by having to take orders from Russia in the light of the Russian rather than the German situation. Their attacks on Socialists, as is usually the case with Communists, were on the whole more aggressive than their attacks on the capitalist parties. No one can deny the sincerity of the Communist opposition to the Nazis. They attested it in plenty of street brawls before the Nazis came to power. Yet there were occasions, as for example when the Prussian Communists joined with the Nazis in an unsuccessful effort to force an election for the removal of the Socialist Cabinet in Prussia, and in certain strikes, when these great enemies made common cause against the Social Democrats. The regular Communist policy was to make it as difficult as possible for a democracy to function in the hope that Communism would be the beneficiary of the resulting indecision and confusion. Such a policy can be justified historically only by success based on a correct calculation of chances. By their incorrect calculation the Communists made Nazi success easier. The party which finally won was the party which by remarkably clever tactics succeeded in using the machinery of German democratic institutions to overthrow democracy without even a *coup d'etat.* The vote which finally gave Hitler power was a vote in which the percentage of desertion from previous Communist electoral strength was far higher than that from the Socialist.

The Communists were at least as unsuccessful as the Socialists in making alliances with those sections of the peasantry and the middle class which the German situation made necessary. In this failure there is a great deal of food for thought for all those who believe that the coöperative commonwealth must be essentially a working-class creation, and who recognize that logically the working class should include all those whose labor of hand or brain keeps the world going. The Social Democrats in Germany did not win important sections of those who had considered themselves as belonging to the middle class. They merely made unsatisfactory coalitions with their parties. The Communists fought them. In the end it was not the followers of Marx but his bitter opponents, the Nazis, who were the beneficiaries of that squeezing-out process which Marx had foreseen as inherent in capitalism and had thought would almost automatically lead to Socialism. The persistence of middle-class psychology and its political strength in Germany are the more extraordinary because Germany's astronomical inflation by wiping out all savings virtually destroyed the old middle class. But the capitalist system still lived to create a new one.

Some things may be controversial in Socialist tactics,

but if the German situation makes anything clear it is that Socialists in America and elsewhere must stop talking as if their continued references to the workers and the proletariat, and their essential trust in the ideals of creative work rather than of ownership, meant that they should limit their appeal and hope to wage workers, and to overall workers at that. The progress of the new technology makes this section of the proletariat less rather than more important. White-collar workers are becoming proportionally more numerous and more important in the economic scheme of things. If they and the young engineers persist in a middle-class ideology and in loyalty to the capitalist system they can break strikes far more easily than in previous periods of capitalism. To give only one illustration: trucks running on hard roads have made railroads far less vital than formerly, and at a time when some knowledge of the automobile is almost universal it is far easier to replace striking truck drivers than railway workers.

German history underlines also the fact that a successful social revolution is not going to be achieved in spite of the farmers. While tariffs and subsidies had gone far in making Germany more nearly self-dependent for foodstuffs than otherwise it would have been, the German peasant was probably less significant politically and economically in the national life than the French peasant and the American farmer. But the failure of Socialists and Communists alike to win the German peasantry or even make a working alliance with any section of it handicapped these proletarian parties tremendously in their race with the Nazis. In spite of which fact it is not uncommon to hear impatient Communists and even Socialists in America talk nonsense about how they will force the farmers into line!

If Germany stands out as a horrible example of what may happen when proletarian parties do not and cannot win those who by every logical consideration ought to count themselves workers, it may in the future furnish the example which will persuade those same workers with middle-class minds how vain is the hope that any reconstruction of the capitalist order will save them. But even this lesson will not impart itself automatically to the farmers, the white-collar workers, and the technicians, who must be definitely won to Socialism if Socialism anywhere in the world is to be the alternative to chaos or Fascism.

One more lesson for both Socialists and Communists is implicit in all that we have been saying about the German situation. It is that the Nazis won because ultimately they forced upon the middle class a temporary unity which the workers never achieved. Even while the German upper and middle classes were divided into multitudes of parties they never hated each other or fought each other so bitterly as the Communists and Socialists in Germany. This division of class-conscious workers concerns not only Germany but the world. It is a problem which we can judge better when we have examined some of its American aspects but we can scarcely close this chapter without some observations on it of international application.

1. It does no good at all to point out the appalling consequences of disunity of the workers in a troubled world unless one can also point out a basis of united action.

2. No organic unity or unity of tactics is possible while Communists cling to their notion of a rigid dictatorship of a party controlled from Russia and by Russia, while Socialists hope, at least in countries like England, France, and America where democracy is not dead, that they may make genuine progress by clarifying the ideals and improving the methods of democracy and applying it to the economic as well as the political life. Even Trotsky has recently reminded his followers of the importance of democratic slogans to the workers of Europe and America in this phase of their development. Perhaps for the future some meeting ground may be found in the conception of democracy and its institutions interpreted definitely and consciously as working-class or proletarian democracy—always remembering the inclusive nature of the working class which I have already discussed.

This democracy need not always insist on thrusting votes on everybody as its first act. Not without trepidation I suggest that the Spanish Revolutionists were not under moral obligation to jeopardize gains made without war by suddenly and indiscriminately bestowing universal suffrage upon women notoriously under the control of priests who were in alliance with the most reactionary class of capitalists and landlords. Was it not highly quixotic to give to women generally a weapon which they had not demanded but which they were likely to use to hurt or destroy a new political social order struggling to life?

In countries where Fascism is already established it is clearly out of the question to use the methods of formal democracy. The revolutionists against this dictatorship cannot win without force though the climactic act by which they win is more likely to be a sudden *coup d'etat* attended by strikes than a long civil war. Under these circumstances to talk about nineteenth-century democracy is meaningless. But to talk about establishing a proletarian democracy rather than a ruthless Communist party dictatorship is anything but meaningless, and work toward it might conceivably be begun by parties in exile and their underground representatives at home.

3. Short of organic unity or a general coalition, Communist and Socialist parties might logically be expected to work out a united front to achieve certain immediate ends upon which both sides are agreed. There is nothing illogical about an international united front against war and Fascism. While the Communist party still believes in the inevitability of new world war and the

possibility of turning it into world revolution, it does not want, and it knows the workers do not want, that war right now. It wants Fascism as little as any Socialist party. Here the thing that stands in the way of unity is neither philosophy nor tactics. It is mutual suspicion. I happen to belong to that group of Socialists, at present in a minority internationally, who believe that the urgency of the situation and the chances of success make it worth while to try boldly and carefully for a united front with Communists upon certain specific issues, especially if and when that united front includes elements which as yet are neither Socialist nor Communist. Tactically I think that the Socialist International and its constituent parties have handled this issue badly and by their mishandling of it allowed the Communists to get some credit for trying to bring about the united front, a credit that their record shows that they do not deserve. But the Socialists of all countries are right in pointing out how difficult it is to have a united front with a party which openly boasts that good faith is a "bourgeois" virtue and which has proclaimed not once but repeatedly in the declarations of its international as well as its national bodies that the purpose of united front maneuvers is to undermine the Socialist parties and destroy Socialist leadership. To this subject of the united front we shall have to return in a later chapter discussing the situation as it exists in America.

But we cannot close this chapter on this note of

gloom. Whatever the mistakes of Communists and Socialists their loyalty is to the coöperative commonwealth
in which alone there is hope for our troubled world.
Their failures have not been failures in the adequacy of
their goal or the glory of their social ideal, but rather in
their plans for making it real. They live and work
among men loaded down with the weight of outworn
institutions, inadequate loyalties, and destructive passions and prejudices. From these things not even the
crusaders for a new order can be wholly exempt. Yet
they are builders of the future. Nor is that future all
unseen save with the eye of faith. We Socialists, even
when we are most insistent that the life of our country
cannot and must not be forced into Russian molds, even
when we are most troubled by the practical and psychological consequences of dictatorship though it be devoted to the noblest ends, rejoice that one great nation
out of the backwardness of Tsaristic oppression and
the horror of war has made such enormous progress in
the harnessing of machinery to the service not of a class
but of the whole company of workers.

CHAPTER VI

THE NEW DEAL IN AMERICA

SINCE the inauguration of Franklin D. Roosevelt on March 4th, 1933, the United States of America has entered with bewildering rapidity on a phase of economic life which is vastly different both from the old individualistic capitalism, which had practically disappeared even while Herbert Hoover was calling it "the American plan," and from the "new" capitalism of great mergers directed by supermen—a capitalism which had been utterly discredited by its own performance. This new economic order is not Fascism, at least not yet, and emphatically it is not Socialism or Communism, although some of its measures look more like a distant approximation of Socialist immediate demands than anything contained in any Democratic platform. What we got is generally known as the *New Deal*, because that vague and rhetorical expression was often on the lips of the President in describing it. In all fairness it must be admitted that he gave more content to his pet phrase than his distant cousin, Theodore Roosevelt, had given to the *Square Deal*, or his Democratic predecessor, Woodrow Wilson, had given to the *New Free-*

dom. One of his admirers, Ernest K. Lindley, has coined for what happened in the crowded months after March 4th the descriptive term, the *Roosevelt Revolution.* It is a term scarcely to be justified even by the author's own account of what happened, except in a limited and qualified sense of the world "revolution." Yet in that sense so definite was the break with the old individualistic capitalist position that the term has meaning.

What has happened and what is likely to happen we shall probably understand better if we begin by considering the historic background rather than a catalogue of legislation. The Presidential campaign of 1932 was fought out in a country deep in the trough of depression. It is now the fashion of some economists and certain critics of the Roosevelt plan to say that recovery was beginning in the Summer of 1932. Certainly, by the Fall of 1932, no one realized it. Mr. Hoover ran on a "do-nothing, let nature take its course" sort of platform. Mr. Roosevelt was going to do something, but was not very specific about what he was going to do. He had earned a reputation as a shrewd politician but there was nothing in his record as governor of New York to warrant any general expectation that he would be a strong man in a crisis. He was clever enough to know that he did not have to commit himself, that the people were so determined to vote Hoover out that his wisest course would be to avoid commitments which might offend his potential supporters. Minority candidates spoke to large audiences and did discuss real issues, but, as I can testify, the very audiences which applauded them made it clear that their set purpose was to eliminate Herbert Hoover. This was done. Franklin Roosevelt was elected by an immense popular and electoral college majority, but with less of a devoted following than some of his defeated Democratic predecessors like William Jennings Bryan or Alfred Emanuel Smith had won.

The long and dangerous stretch between the popular election and the inauguration, a stretch of time now wisely shortened by the adoption of the twentieth amendment to the Constitution, saw conditions go from bad to worse. The essential unsoundness of the American banking system, or rather the forty-nine systems, state and federal, proved to be quite beyond the power of Mr. Hoover's Reconstruction Finance Corporation to remedy by pouring in loans without adequate security. In February, 1933, bank failures became epidemic. The extent of unemployment was estimated all the way from thirteen to seventeen millions. Relief was woefully inadequate. Farm prices were generally below the cost of production. I found in that month that a favorite story in Illinois had to do with a farmer who took his corn into a local market, sold it for ten cents a bushel, and then looked around to see what such vast wealth would buy. After careful shopping he came out of a five- and ten-cent store with a corn-cob pipe. One bushel of corn had equalled one corn-cob pipe! Nevertheless, farmers had this advantage over unemployed workers in the city: they usually had a roof over their heads and some food in the cellar. The farmers had organized spontaneously, and by direct action and by a boycott of any man who bought or rented a farm from which one of their number had been dispossessed, they had greatly slowed up the process of foreclosure or eviction. This action of the farmers, some demonstrations of the unemployed, a few riots and strikes—amazingly few, all things considered—were the chief outward expressions of mingled discontent and despair which covered America. Nowhere was any leadership. Congress and the outgoing President were at loggerheads. Great industrialists and bankers were discredited not only by the depression itself but by partial revelations that began to come out concerning such colossal failures as the Kreuger and Insull collapses and the piratical conduct of great bankers in floating foreign and domestic securities, the unsoundness of which they should have known and told.

I travelled widely that black Winter and testify from personal observation that the people were ripe for riot. If they remained patient it was partly because they were willing to see what the new Administration would do. Yet at that period they had surprisingly little confidence in it, despite the huge majority they had given it. The people, I say, were ripe for riot, but emphatically not for constructive revolution. For that, both an ideal and effective organization were lacking.

Events moved faster and faster. By March first it was a race between the coming of Inauguration Day and the complete collapse of the banking system. Mr. Roosevelt won in a neck-to-neck finish. He was inaugurated before the banks closed and in time to close them. Will Rogers wrote him a letter which voiced the desire of the American people. It read about like this: "Mr. President, do something, if only it is to burn down the Capitol"—or was it the White House? Mr. Roosevelt proceeded to do something and possibly burning the Capitol would have been as sensible as some of the things he did—for instance, the destruction of pigs in a hungry world!

I dwell on the gravity of the situation, because men have such short memories. Bankers who were glad enough to be saved in March, and a Chamber of Commerce which actually petitioned the President to come to its rescue were, by December, 1933, inclined to think that everything would have been all right if only Mr. Roosevelt had left them alone and the processes of recovery which had set in in the Summer of 1932 had been allowed to continue! Those processes of recovery, be it observed, had not made any nation in Europe prosperous or content. They were completely frustrated by the banking collapse in the United States, for which bad laws were less to blame than the extraordinarily short-sighted greed of bankers themselves and the magnitude of the gambling orgy in which almost all commercial banks had participated, and in which some of the great bankers were leaders. Moreover, it must be remembered that England, at least, was buttressed against spontaneous revolt by a far more adequate system of social insurance relief than existed in the United States, where, through three long years a dominant capitalist class had insisted upon treating unemployment as primarily a problem for charity. Whether what Mr. Roosevelt did was good, bad, or indifferent, it was at least action which temporarily restored hope and confidence and lifted the country out of the depths of depression.

In the process he changed the form of capitalism, and that not merely for the emergency, to the duration of which many of his measures were directed. It was his merit that he and the advisers whom he chose were intelligent enough to know that the old *laissez-faire* or *individualistic* capitalism was dead. They did not, like Herbert Hoover, hymn its praises as a living force what time they cast upon its grave such great stones as the Reconstruction Finance Corporation. But Mr. Roosevelt did not kill *capitalism*. His first achievement was symbolic. He took over a completely broken-down banking system. In hundreds, if not thousands, of cases banks which might be considered still this side of bankruptcy,

were so near the line that the equity of stockholders
was wiped out. He could have nationalized banking
with the public behind him.

Under the capitalist system, if this banking chain had
been nationally owned it would not necessarily have
been socialized. It would have been socialized only if
the control of it and of credit were directed consciously
to setting up a system of production for use and not
profit. But Mr. Roosevelt, who to be sure was not
elected to socialize or even to nationalize banks, did
nothing of the sort. He patched up the system and gave
it back to the bankers to see if they could ruin it again.
His Comptroller of the Currency openly commended
the inadequate and rather dubious federal guarantee of
deposits up to twenty-five hundred dollars, by telling the
Texas bankers that they ought to prefer this system to
public ownership! At the end of 1933 the chief result
of the New Deal in banking was the restored confidence
in banks, but not any such organization of them as
would make them as safe as the banks of Canada or
England. Government control over them was greater,
but by no means did it amount to a social direction of
credit and banking. Wall Street had not abdicated. If,
to use Mr. Roosevelt's figure of speech in his inaugural
address, he had driven the money changers out of the
temple, he had soon let them back, washed a bit behind
the ears, wearing for a time at least their Sabbath rai-

ment, and watched more carefully. But back they were, some of them in the choir, for a time at least, singing praises to their savior.

It may be that events will yet force the Administration to take more drastic action in regard to the banks. It is an open secret that large areas of America are without banking facilities. Who will go in, the government or private bankers? Since for the immediate present there will be no great profit in going in, the government may have to act. But if the Administration is forced by such considerations to some advance in the nationalization of banking, it must be remembered that Mr. Roosevelt set the tone of his New Deal not by taking over the banks, which might have been a step toward Socialism, but by subsidizing them for the benefit of the private owners. This is essentially state capitalism.

Exactly the same principle was applied to the railroads. Under makeshift legislation the President appointed an able man, Mr. Joseph Eastman, as coördinator, with the avowed purpose of restoring the railroads to a condition where they could again pay profits to absentee stockholders. The whole process must be largely at the expense of the workers and tends to increase the cost or the difficulty of ultimately acquiring the railroads, as most assuredly the Government must. To agriculture Mr. Roosevelt gave the shot in the arm of a subsidy imposed at cost to the consumer. George

N. Peek, then Administrator of the Adjustment Act and still high in Administration favor, candidly declared its essentially capitalist purpose in the hearing on the Grain Exchange Codes on September 9, 1933. Said he:

Unless we can get these farm prices up—I don't mean after the farmer has sold his grain, but before he has sold his grain—I anticipate that you will face legislation next Winter which may make what we are talking about now fade into insignificance compared with the restrictive provisions that will be placed upon you.

I say that with all the candor in the world, because I am interested primarily in preserving the social order under which we have all grown and prospered to a greater or less degree.

With the number of strikes all over the country, the coal strike in Pennsylvania, the milk strike in New York, the lumber strike throughout the entire lumber region, and others, if you don't keep the farmer *conservative*, then he is going with the other crowd. He isn't going to stand still, and be dispossessed of his home and property through no fault of his own.

It is in the interest of the nation, I think, that everything that can be done shall be done to keep him *conservative*. He is not going to remain so under conditions —and I don't say imposed by you or anybody else in particular—such as have existed during the last few years." [Italics mine.]

When it came to working out codes for industry under the National Industrial Recovery Act, Mr. Roosevelt did indeed state that wages ought to come before profit, but the codes in no way challenge the principle of private ownership of great resources and the immense tools of production. Instead, Mr. Roosevelt at that period talked much of partnership between government, the workers, and industry, which in reality meant between the government, workers, and absentee owners. What was the logical basis of such a partnership this shrewd and bold opportunist never attempted to say. Actually the partnership he established is scarcely more enduring than that of the lion and the lamb who might lie down together in the common misery of sea-sickness, but only until the lion found his sea legs or the storm subsided. Of all the President's plans, only the Tennessee Valley Authority development of the power and resources of that valley for use rather than private profit could be called Socialist, and the fate of this and its ultimate influence were a bit doubtful, despite the ability of the men in control, in the capitalist setting of the rest of American industry which the New Deal has not changed.

To say that the Roosevelt Revolution, in so far as it was a revolution at all, was a revolution from *laissez-faire* to state capitalism, is not to deny the magnitude of some of its achievements or the considerable measure of social idealism behind them. In Akron, Ohio, and St. Louis, Missouri, and for all I know in other towns, editors did a pretty competent job in showing that certain features of the Roosevelt program far more nearly resembled the Socialist immediate demands than his own platform. Socialists had demanded the thirty-hour week in industry; the workers got a thirty-five- or forty-hour week in most of the codes—some ran as high as fifty-four hours! Socialists had demanded at least ten billion dollars for public works and direct unemployment relief; the country got all together some $3,800,000,000 in federal appropriation for this end. Socialists had demanded an end of sweat-shops and child labor; the country got the abolition of the worst of sweat-shop conditions under the codes, and of child labor in factories, if not in the beet sugar and cotton fields and the vending of newspapers.

It will be observed that even in immediate demands the Roosevelt Revolution only distantly approximated what Socialists had asked. It is more important to observe that the essential thing about the Socialist platform has always been its purpose and its goal rather than its immediate demands. Socialists ask certain things in order that the workers may have strength to go on to take power away from private owners of productive goods. The Roosevelt program makes concessions to workers in order to keep them quiet a while longer and so stabilize the power of private owners. The essence of the Socialist position is its philosophy, a philosophy of social ownership of the great natural resources, the principal means of production and distribution, and their management according to plan for the use of the whole company of the people, and not for the profit of the few. It was, the President's admirers told us, his virtue that he was not cumbered with a philosophy and therefore he could more easily find out what play would work. These eulogists did not share the Socialist fear that, lacking in philosophy and a sense of direction, the quarter-back might make some bold play only to discover that, as happened in a famous game in California, he had scored his points for the enemy team behind the wrong goal line.

From these generalizations let us turn to some examination of the outstanding features of the New Deal. It is a temptation, which in the limits of this book we must resist, to examine the brilliant generalship by which Mr. Roosevelt worked out his program and persuaded Congress to give him power. It gives one a new measure of faith in the possibility of leadership in a democracy even under a rigid constitution and a judicial oligarchy. The powers given to the President were very great, but in no true sense did they amount to setting up a dictatorship. They were democratically granted and kept under sufficient democratic control. Before the optimistic radical rejoices overmuch, however, he should remember that these powers have not yet met the test of the Supreme Court; that both the negotiation of the codes and the effectiveness of their enforcement have been impaired because of the Administration's well-founded belief that its strength was dependent, in as far as possible, on persuasion rather than on legal authority. It hesitated to put its powers to the test, which even if in the end it resulted in victory would tie up its machinery during months of emergency. Finally, it must be remembered, that so much power was so easily granted to Mr. Roosevelt under stress of emergency precisely because he was regarded as the savior of something or the restorer of something, rather than the creator of the cooperative commonwealth. Was not his most far-reaching legislation passed in the name of the national recovery of that prosperity which in reality the workers had never had? But for our present purpose the study of the Roosevelt technique is less important than the study of his program.

After the first harmony born of the crisis had passed, it became fashionable for Mr. Roosevelt's critics on the right to point out the inconsistencies of his program. Apparently he had improvised important parts of it as he went along. It is true that at first he had insisted upon caution and sound banking, only later on to urge banks to liberalize credit. He balanced the regular budget by drastic economies, only to expand the emergency budget, so that by the end of a year the debt is likely to pass its height during the World War. He had cut the salaries of federal employees, in the case of substitute postal clerks to a sweat-shop level, only to urge private employers above all things to pay better wages. But some of these contradictions were more apparent than real and all of them were superficial. In sum total the Roosevelt Revolution tried to do right by everybody, but always without changing the underlying system. Before election, Mr. Roosevelt had talked a good deal about the "forgotten man," who was apparently a cousin to the "little man" to whom Mussolini and Hitler had appealed. The working out of the codes, whatever Mr. Roosevelt's intentions, increased the difficulties of the forgotten man or the little man. The big corporation was better able to arrange its shifts and meet the provisions of hours without downright dishonesty to the code. The new legislation simply accentuated the inevitable capitalist drift to concentration in its freezing out of the little man. But on the way Mr. Roosevelt did what he could for his old friend, the forgotten man, by putting through Congress a rigid securities act for the better protection of Wall Street's little lambs. This legislation, which the President said embodied the sentiment, "Let the seller beware," was designed for the better protection of investors, especially little investors, not of workers. It was a family affair within capitalist circles for protecting the poor fish from their cannibal relations. In like fashion, Mr. Roosevelt tried to come to the help of the small, but not the smallest, home owners. It cannot be said, however, that his provisions for the relief of the mortgage-burdened farmer and home owner were conspicuously successful.

I quote from a summary I have previously used in a pamphlet, *Workers and the New Deal:*

HOME OWNERS' LOAN ACT

The much-heralded Home Owners' Loan Act has developed three important defects.

First, the holder of the mortgage must be *persuaded* to accept government bonds, which are guaranteed only as to interest,[1] in exchange for his mortgage. In practice this has proven very difficult.

Second, building and loan companies and many banks and trust companies are not permitted by state laws to invest in this type of security.

Third, the requirement that such mortgage refinancing be limited to 80 per cent of the present fair value of the property has also given considerable difficulty. The kind of homes which need refinancing are not in this class. The real problem in home and farm refinancing is that the mortgage debt is often greater than the present value of the property. The only solution for this problem is the forced scaling down of the principal. It remains to be seen whether the new farm and home mortgage adjustment committees can accomplish this scaling down without any other power than that of persuasion.

The developments to date have indicated a complete failure of this act in all but one respect; namely, producing jobs for deserving Democrats.

There are forty-eight offices and 208 branch offices employing 10,000 people. According to Chairman John

---

[1] The guarantee of principal as well as interest under the recent amendment to the law will lessen this difficulty and probably increase the burden on the general public.

H. Fahey, the Home Owners Loan Corporation had made by November 10, 6,942 loans totalling $20,275,125.00. In other words, during its first two months of operation, the corporation had loaned about 1 per cent of the total money available under the act and had made about two loans for every three employees.

Even if the machinery is speeded up, not much will happen except that Uncle Sam will take some selective risks by aiding a comparatively few of those burdened with debt. And the strain on the private lenders will be eased!

The heart of the Roosevelt program lies in three measures: (1) The Agricultural Adjustment Act, to which the rider giving the President vast powers of inflation is attached; (2) the National Industrial Recovery Act, which was coupled with (3) a bill appropriating $3,300,000,000 for public works. Another $500,-000,000 was appropriated for relief.

In the first chapter of this book I have referred to the Agricultural Adjustment Act as the greatest satire that could be penned on the civilization that was alleged to make it necessary. In essence it was a bill to re-create artificially a scarcity which centuries of struggle had at last taught man to conquer. It proposed to pay farmers not to produce and to pay them out of a tax on processing, which must be collected from the consumer. It could be justified only as an emergency measure in a world where the economic nationalism of tariffs made it all but impossible for American farmers to produce for an effective demand, and confined them to a home market suffering from depression.

In so far as the bill tends to create one price for agricultural products at home and a lower price abroad, it invites the nations to charge America with "dumping" goods, and that charge always embitters international relations. That it has not yet been raised more loudly against us is perhaps due to the fact that our currency depreciation has in effect raised the exorbitant Hawley-Smoot rates about sixty per cent against foreign goods in America, and over any long period we cannot sell even at prices that look like dumping, unless we buy.

The long and short of the law to date is that it has added an average of about forty dollars per farm family in income for 1933. This has been very unevenly distributed, because it has gone only to farmers that specialize in staples like cotton, wheat, corn and hogs. In the case of the miserably poor crop-sharers of the South, chronically held in serfdom to the landlords by their debts, the law operates to drive them out as homeless wanderers. A law reducing acreage and paying the landlord for it can have no other effect. Estimates run from 500,000 to 800,000 families which face this fate with no reasonable hope of absorption into industry. Even the proposal to put submarginal land back into publicly owned forests—a proposal in itself essentially sound and long advocated by Socialists—will have this effect and be hurtful rather than helpful to this generation, save as it is accompanied by definite provision for the care of families dispossessed, until under a new economic program they can be absorbed in industry. (By one of those paradoxes not uncommon in the New Deal, the Administration which is thus reducing the number of farm families in large areas is elsewhere experimenting by putting some unemployed on subsistence farms!)

Meanwhile farmers are discovering that the processing tax is not only passed on, as expected, to the consumers by the middle-men and processors, but to some extent passed back to the farmers by reducing what they are offered. And the rest of us are discovering—what we ought to have known—that there is no guarantee at all of reducing output proportionately to the reduction of acreage. The best lands can be cultivated intensively and make up the difference. There are lots of farmers like the man who told the inquirer: "The first $1,000 I got for plowing under my cotton I put into fertilizer for the rest of the land. It needed it!"

Secretary Wallace and his principal advisers are high-minded and competent. Mr. Wallace has talked with unusual candor of the necessity of making up our minds about economic nationalism or internationalism. But the law which gives him such vast powers solves nothing and creates an immense potential subsidy-seeking bloc to add its voice to the voices of its predecessors, which the tariff has created in bedeviling politics. Nothing fundamental is done about landlordism and exploited tenantry—over fifty per cent in rich agricultural states; a terrific and unscientific load of taxation; the mortgage burden, and the wastes in the whole process of marketing under the profit system. A. A. A. may be a pillar under the New Deal; it is no foundation for a new world. It postpones and ultimately intensifies evils it does not solve. Even in the emergency a more reasonable policy would have bought up, not destroyed, cotton and pigs, using the surplus to relieve want and hunger at home and destitution and famine abroad—let us say, in China.

The National Industrial Recovery Act is itself more constructive, though leadership under it has been less thoughtful and expert. It was welcomed by most employers, because it was a substitute for the Black Bill, which imposed a mandatory thirty-hour week on industry, and gave them a chance to form associations without worrying too much about anti-trust legislation and to eliminate some of the grossest wastes of cutthroat competition. It was welcomed by Labor, because it encouraged organization and collective bargaining and gave promise of increased employment by shortening hours of labor, and at the same time raising wages and so increasing the spending power of the masses—which is the spending power that matters.

These promises were only partially fulfilled. America's

great boom in industrial activity came not because of
the codes but in anticipation of them. Production in
many lines speeded up to get ahead of the introduction
of the codes. Later it slowed down. The indexes of
business activity dropped almost steadily after the June
and July boom through the rest of the year. Employment was increased, but at the beginning of November
some ten to eleven million unemployed faced another
winter without any social insurance and without any
direct cash unemployment allotment. During November, according to the A. F. of L. estimate, unemployment actually increased by over three hundred thousand.
The springs of private charity had run dry. The funds
of most cities and states neared exhaustion. In spite
of N. R. A. and the rest of the New Deal there were
more unemployed in America than in the whole of
Europe.[1]

The total wage fund was, of course, increased over
that of March, 1933. The lowest sweat-shop wages
were fairly well abolished, at least unless and until inflation should wipe out all the gains the codes had
made for the least well-paid. The Administration did
not suggest, and Labor did not demand, the insertion
in the codes of a provision that automatically wages

[1] After this paragraph was in type, Frances Perkins, Secretary of
Labor, announced a further decline of employment in December. Employment stood at 70 per cent of 1926, regarded as normal, while pay-
rolls had dropped to 49.8 per cent, lower than last July, when N.R.A.
became effective. Employment was at the July level when, thanks to
machinery, production was almost 100 per cent.

fixed in the codes would rise as the index of the cost of living rose. By the end of the year the employing class, as a whole, had recovered much of its arrogance. Henry Ford successfully defied the N. R. A. on collective bargaining. Employers found ways to make maximum wages approximate the minimum set in the codes. Chiselling became a fine art, more generally practiced than bootlegging under the Eighteenth Amendment. The N. R. A. was discovered to have few, if any, teeth. Complaints mounted high but action was rare. The machinery of complaint itself for the worker in non-unionized industries was difficult, costly in time and perhaps of the job itself. Altogether, the average American, fortunate enough to have a job above the sweatshop level, gained little or nothing by the codes. He began to suspect that work sharing, the old Hoover principle in a new dress, had more to do with the increase in the number of jobs than increased spending power. He learned that merely to shorten hours did not correspondingly increase the number of jobs, because there was always the possibility of introducing new labor machinery or speeding up the old. He heard stories such as that of the manufacturer on the train who told his friend that under the codes he had actually saved in wages, and he began to believe, perhaps mistakenly, that manufacturer was typical. Even where vigorous union organization took advantage of the codes, there was one of the most extraordinary declines in enthusiasm for them that I have ever seen in public opinion on any subject. This decline took place, roughly speaking, between the middle or end of September and the first of December.

Now for all this there was a reason inherent in the limitation of the Roosevelt plan. Of themselves, the codes made little direct attack on the maldistribution of the national income, which is the root of our trouble. Without that attack they could not produce increased spending power. This would probably have been the case even if Mr. Roosevelt and his picturesque N. R. A. Administrator, General Hugh Johnson, had dared to go further in raising wages and reducing hours. They could not have gone further without scaring those other partners, the beneficiaries of the sacred institutions of profit, rent, and interest. These institutions they did not touch. They did not so much as seek to introduce a general economic plan for the chaos of the profit system. They tried to build a house by letting each individual or each set of room-mates plan one room without so much as a blue print to show how the house was to be put together. They tried to fight the great enemy, poverty, with an army, each regiment of which had its own manual of arms—and pretty poor some of them were— but without any general staff or general strategy. How could they have done much else under the capitalist system? It is very hard to plan for what you do not own or to bring order into an industry, the moving power in which is a desire to make profit. The coal code, for example, did better the condition of West Virginia serfs, but it could not cure a sick industry which could be cured only by a program of nationalization. The codes were of uneven merit, and the variation in hours enormous. Some of them conflicted with others. A. A. A. and N. R. A. did not drive well in double harness. The farmer bitterly complained when he had to pay twice what he formerly paid for his overalls without a corresponding increase in agricultural prices. If A. A. A. and N. R. A. had worked together, something might have been done in the dramatic strike of cotton pickers in California in October, 1933, to break the yoke of finance corporations over the farmers, so that they could more easily have paid living wages to the pickers. A. A. A. kept out and N. R. A. was not effective.[1] Mean-

[1] As time went on it was the business interests, at first suspicious of the codes, which came to love them best. Under cloak of the Administration's desire to raise the price level and abolish cut-throat competition, they began through the code authorities and in the name of determining reasonable costs to impose upon industry what were virtually fixed prices. These prices, fixed through "open price" associations and otherwise gave to the better placed business interests handsome profits and no protection to consumers. Indeed, it was only after this chapter was written that consumers' representation in Washington became anything but a fifth wheel to the coach. Now, thanks to some strengthening of machinery and to the airing in the Senate of the dangers of monopoly control, there is a chance that the administration of N. R. A. may set up some controls over a process of price fixing, open or disguised, of which the consumer is more truly a victim than the small-scale producer in whose name some of the Senators have been fighting. But the most interesting part of the story is that nobody yet has found an automatic formula under our present system which will at one and the same time preserve profit, wipe out cut-throat competition, prevent monopoly, and guarantee a fair price to the producer which will not gouge the consumer. The ablest and most disinterested administrators will be unable to accomplish these incompatible objectives under the codes.

while cases multiplied in which N. R. A. was used as an excuse for enjoining strikes, forbidding picketing, and interfering in the name of the government with the workers' right to make and join their own unions.

These difficulties, it cannot be too strongly insisted, are inherent in capitalism, not primarily in the codes as codes. Before the end of 1933 it was evident that the chief use of the N. R. A. to Labor was the encouragement it gave it to organize and bargain collectively; and even here there was the danger that if labor could not take advantage of this encouragement in proper fashion it would become a strait-jacket for it. With regard to the whole New Deal it was clear that great as were the legislative achievements of the Roosevelt Administration it would have to do more and go further if we were not to sink hopelessly in a third phase of depression.

Mr. Roosevelt's resourcefulness, which had already exceeded anything of which his earlier record gave promise, was by no means exhausted. Early in his Administration he had come around to the idea of "priming the pump" by liberal expenditures for public works. Socialists had commended this idea in the campaign of 1932, but they had taken care to point out that the analogy of the capitalist system in this stage of its development to a pump which only needed priming before it should again gush forth with living water, was decidedly faulty. Our pump did, indeed, need priming, but it was in such a rickety condition that no priming could have more than a partial and temporary success. Even Mr. Roosevelt believed that the pump needed some minor improvements and so had coupled his public works program with the National Recovery Act. He borrowed a little red paint from his neighbor's pot to touch up the pump!

Not only did the National Recovery Act prove inefficient in fixing up the pump but the amount and character of the priming was inadequate. The three billion, three hundred million dollars allotted for public works was spent slowly, partly because of the difficulties of preparing proper plans and getting them to work honestly and efficiently. But even if'the entire sum could have been spent rapidly it would not have brought the amount spent in the United States for public works by all governmental agencies, municipal, state, and national, up to the level of good years, and it left the general level of production, public and private, far below the level of construction which had been a factor in such prosperity as we had enjoyed.

It is now generally agreed, even by conservative authorities, that the most useful form of public works would be the provision of decent housing for that quarter of our population now housed in shacks and slums below the level of what is decent in a nation of builders. During the campaign of 1932, and with redoubled efforts during the dark days between Mr. Roosevelt's election and inauguration, I pushed the Socialist demand for a program of housing under public, non-profit-making authorities, set up by coöperation between the federal, state and municipal governments. I urged that four billion dollars be allotted as a first install-ment on such a program, most of which under proper plans could be repaid to the federal government, since public housing can be made to carry most of its own costs. In so far as the theory of priming the pump is valid, public housing would be the best of such priming, and there would be few better methods of fighting dis-ease, vice, gangsterism, and the general ugliness of much of our modern life than a program which would do for the American countryside, as well as for cities, something like as good a job as Vienna has done for her workers. It represents progress that the Public Works Administration is taking an interest in lending money to limited dividend companies which cannot do a proper job and to publicly owned housing corpora-tions which can. The beginning is cautious and inade-quate. Much will depend upon the initiative of cities. It is gratifying to see that Mayor LaGuardia in New York and his backers have at last taken a fairly definite stand for municipal housing—a stand which Major LaGuardia avoided almost as deftly as Mayor Walker, when I challenged them both in 1929. The danger is that real estate owners and money lenders will now de-feat, by flank attack, a proposal which they dare not meet head on. Housing requires more than the building of a few or many model apartments. It requires an overhauling of our whole system of taxation and mortgages, and it certainly requires city and county planning to achieve proper benefit. It will be interesting to see how far the national Administration will go in urging this sort of priming.

Other efforts to prime the pump, such as the effort to expand credit and make it cheaper, and the mild inflation which followed our departure from the gold standard, also proved inadequate to the task of reëmploying the unemployed. The Administration did not have enough funds on hand for direct relief in an emergency, where the national government clearly had to bear the brunt of the burden. In its emergency legislation it had refused to consider social insurance for which there was no time to build up reserves, or direct cash allotment for the unemployed, or the taking over of factories in which they could be set to producing for themselves. (Any decent plan for relieving unemployment with the maximum of efficiency with regard for the self-respect of the unemployed, would involve a judicious combination of the latter two methods and a very sparing use of made work, except such as could be brought under the normal category of useful work.) The Administration resorted, instead, to two methods of its own to meet this emergency. It bought considerable stores of food from the farmers' surplus to dole out to the unemployed and it set up a plan for work relief with the funds, most of which it got from the sum allotted to public works. The amount thus made available was supposed to care for two million workers for three months. This was about a fifth of the number unemployed and less than half the number already on relief rolls. Actually, this number was exceeded by the end of the year. C. W. A. and C. W. S., which administer the fund, were the principal factors in holding the situation together. With all their faults it was clear that for an indefinite future they would have to be continued, unless a better substitute could be found. C. W. A. pay (sometimes in excess of N. R. A. rates, to the disgrace of the latter) is the kind of bone that can't be taken away without trouble!

Nevertheless, made work primes no pumps. Neither food, doles, nor work relief can restore prosperity or do much more than avert starvation or riot. But the Civil Works Administration deserves credit for trying hard and intelligently to find as much work as possible at which to put men and women who need feel themselves no longer recipients of relief but useful workers. The faults in the machinery, some of them serious, are not at the top but in the local administrations, with their unsatisfactory mixture of politicians, charity workers and would-be philanthropists, inherited from the days when unemployment relief in America was the worst and most demoralizing form of dole.

Professor Graham of Princeton has recently suggested an interesting substitute for work, even good work, under C. W. A. and P. W. A. He proposes that the government use its money to buy say twenty per cent of the normal or current production of all kinds of storable manufactured goods. These contracts would immediately start work on a big scale. The government would then sell back to the industries at the same price these goods, as they found markets, for which presumably increased employment would create a demand. The process could be repeated more or less indefinitely, and Professor Graham believes it would be the best form of priming the pump yet devised. The objections to this plan are these: (1) It does not follow that we need to increase purchase of goods in the same proportion as they are now purchased in our crazy society to get prosperity. After the first purchase, Professor Graham provides for no further purchase of goods that do not move. But the government will be stuck with what it has. From this angle it would be better, as Socialists have argued, to grant a flat cash unemployment allowance, and let the unemployed, by their own buying, stimulate those industries which really need such stimulus. (2) Unless there is to be a deliberate curtailment of the use of machinery or a far better thought-out reduction of hours than we yet have, these government orders would be filled by goods produced by the more efficient use of machinery without employing the old number of workers. (3) The worst feature of the program is that at no point does it lessen the rewards of ownership as compared to the rewards of labor. The factories which get the government orders will have to meet the same charges of profit, rent, and interest. The workers, as consumers, will not have the use of the whole of each dollar which the government has put into the order. That, of course, is a fault inherent in capitalism and in any system for priming the capitalist pump. Public housing comes nearer to blazing a new trail if it is so handled as to reduce or eliminate the tolls now taken by private landowners and money lenders. This reduction would be great if the government were to meet the initial costs in whole or in part by treasury notes, secured by the value of the property but bearing no interest. Whether that would mean inflation to any unwholesome extent we can better make up our minds when we have discussed that controversial theme.

In point of fact the old family remedy, inflation, is about all that the capitalist system has left to try. To be sure capitalist doctors had never agreed about this remedy. Some of them always insisted that it was no true remedy and that the restoration of health could come only through the crude surgery of deflation, bankruptcy, and foreclosure. Nor did the inflationist doctors agree among themselves. I have learned to count the day lost whose low descending sun has seen no new plan for saving the country by inflation, called to my attention by public print or private letter. The doctors do not agree. Which is why the canny Dr. Roosevelt persuaded Congress to give him power to try almost any method of inflation, doubtless in the hope that he could prescribe small enough doses to keep the patient satisfied and prevent such a jag as had accompanied inflation on historic occasions, only to be followed by a terrible hang-over.

But by November, after the business index had been dropping pretty steadily almost every week, and the restlessness of farmers had shown itself in the abortive but significant farmers' holiday strike and six mid-Western governors had demanded a gigantic price-fixing program for agriculture, it was clear that something had to be done. Indeed, it would have been clear that something would have to be done if for no other reason from a consideration of the burden of debt, public and private, under which America staggered. In a study of the debt situation, made under the auspices of the Twentieth Century Fund, the experts agree that in 1932 the debt service absorbed twenty per cent of the national income. In the black month of February, 1933, an eminent economist gave it as his informal opinion that if the holders of bonds, mortgages, and other indebtedness certificates could collect at their face value they would collect more than the monetary value of the wealth of the United States.

Now with the increase of the price level and of the volume of business it is possible that the first year of the New Deal will show some relative decline in the percentage of the national income absorbed in debt service. It will not show an absolute decline, because of the steady increase of the public debt—the deficit for the current fiscal year reaches the appalling total of $7,000,000,000, and it certainly will not show Mr. Bassett Jones' required one to one relation between the rate of increase of debt and the rate of increase of production, unless within the next few months it can wipe out a large part of the existing debt. On the contrary, the President's bold budget message gives us reason to expect an increase of the federal debt to more than thirty-one billion dollars, and little reason to share his hope that it will reach its height by the end of 1935.

Historically, every form of predatory society, and most certainly capitalism, is always wiping out or arbitrarily reducing debt. If this were not so the horrendous figures of Coin Harvey and others, which show what compound interest is doing to us, would more often be statements of actual fact instead of what might have been. The methods by which debts can be reduced and have been reduced, under capitalism, include: (1) Outright repudiation, which the modern capitalist state tries to avoid or mask because of its destructive effects on confidence; (2) deflationary methods, which in this case mean that both debtor and creditor submit to losses through processes of bankruptcy and foreclosure; and (3) inflation which, if carried far enough as it was in Germany, can practically wipe out the internal debt or can reduce it, as was the case in the bourgeois Republic of France, as much as four-fifths, by a process of first inflating money and then stabilizing it at a fraction of its original value. The extremes of either inflation or deflation mean ruin. If long continued they would result in actual economic death. On the whole, the inflationary method of reducing debt is psychologically pleasanter to more people and less likely to result in popular uprising or plain economic paralysis than the method of wholesale bankruptcy and foreclosure.

There is one other method of reducing debt far more scientific, equable and merciful than those which I have listed. It is the capital levy; that is, a carefully graduated tax, similar in nature to the inheritance tax, but assessed against the wealth of the living. Such a tax is not capricious as is every other method of debt reduction. It falls equably on all holders of wealth. It does not destroy one wealthy class only to make another. It can be begun at a level which does not mean the ruthless sweeping away of the savings of the little men. It may be supplemented by reducing capital structure in some industries and lowering the rate of interest on debt, but these measures cannot take the place of the capital levy in an orderly program of wiping out debts.

Writing in 1930 I recognized a capital levy as one form of taxation useful in a process of socialization, but because of constitutional difficulties in its way I did not then think a capital levy necessary if income and inheritance taxes were properly used. With the continuance of the depression I became convinced that the capital levy was necessary in order to deal as fairly and as painlessly as possible with our debt burden, and as such I advocated it strongly in the campaign of 1932, to the alarm of thousands of people who refused to face the fact that debts would have to be reduced if we did not want general collapse. To the case for a capital levy in the process of socialization I shall return. Here in the discussion of the New Deal, I can only insist that not all the economists in Christendom, plus the bankers, plus Al Smith, plus the Crusaders, and the officialdom of the American Legion, with Matt Woll thrown in for good measure, can stop some sort of inflation, unless they can show something else to do about this burden of debt. It does little good to talk about "rubber dollars" or "boloney dollars" in a country where, in March, 1933, the dollar would purchase twice as much as in 1926, whereas by November the President's policy had already helped to bring it down to 146, taking the 1926 dollar as 100.

Readers of this book will have a great advantage over the author in knowing what will happen in the war of the dollar which has begun so lustily while I write. I can only point out that from the beginning, of necessity, the success of the New Deal was bound up with a rise in prices, which meant some stimulation to a system of money and credit which had suffered sorely from deflation. The first stimulus came when the President abandoned the gold standard—as I had predicted that probably he must when he was only a candidate professing to love it as much as Herbert Hoover himself. Merely to go off the gold standard, however, in a country where most prices are fixed in a domestic market, does not necessarily mean much inflation. So the President tried, like Mr. Hoover before him, to stimulate bank credit in which and not in currency the great deflation had taken place. This effort was not successful, because business demands were sluggish and bankers feared risk. More successful was reflation by means of reopening banks. Then came the gold purchase plan with its deliberate effort to cheapen the dollar by purchasing gold in the world market. This soon proved what ought to have been evident from the first; namely, that it was likely to be more satisfactory to the inflationists politically than economically. Professor Warren's now famous theory did not work out. Prices did not rise proportionately to the increase in dollars of the price of gold.

We are slowly learning that even in a society which persists in regarding gold as the logical money, although most nations are off the gold standard, the price of gold and the quantity of gold do not of themselves by any process of manipulation decide whether we shall have inflation and if so, how much. There are other factors to be considered. Normally in America the ratio of bank credit to actual currency is around ten to one and bank credit can be immensely swollen or contracted within the limits set by the amount of gold which banks, in a gold-standard country, are compelled to keep in reserve. We had a terrific and wholly unjustified inflation of credits in the boom period, while we were still on the gold standard. This is something that Al Smith forgot. We could have another such inflation if we were to go back on the gold standard at the wrong time, in the wrong way, or with the wrong value of the dollar. From a strictly economic standpoint it is hard to bring about inflation in a country with great productive capacity and great consumers' wants solely by increasing the amount of currency. That has been increased by something like $1,800,000,000 since 1926. But in the meanwhile the velocity with which it circulates has fallen and bank credits have shrunk by something like ten billion.

The wrong sort of tinkering with gold or silver or the operation of printing presses to turn out paper money may do economic harm, especially in international trade and in that national irritation which follows wars of currencies. But it would take a tremendous output of printing presses in America actually to produce such harm as followed the German inflation. It must be remembered that at that time the whole of German economic and industrial life was disorganized by French occupation of the Ruhr. We have no equivalent for that. We do, however, have a situation in which inflation might get out of hand and where the uncertainty about it is very demoralizing. Fear of inflation or of the beginning of inflation may have a disastrous psychological effect and actually produce a further contraction of bank credits, with the result of a greatly increased demand for inflation of currency in a big way.

This is not a book primarily about money and credit. Much less is it a contribution to the war between inflationists and anti-inflationists. That is essentially a capitalist war between two schools of doctors, both trying to restore King Profit to health. The whole system of money, banking, and credit, indeed the whole price system, would be radically changed in a Socialist society. Even in the transition to a Socialist society, Socialism may make an increasing use of a scheme like Major Douglas' much-discussed Social Dividend. That conception has value despite the absurd anti-Semitism which accompanies his statement of it. But it is unreasonable for Major Douglas or anybody else to imagine that any society can or will suddenly take its system of money and credit out of the hands of interest collectors and profit makers and organize it under ideals diametrically opposed to theirs, except as a part of a process of asserting social ownership of natural resources and great machinery and their operation for use, not profit.

Mr. Fred Henderson in his brilliant little books on *Money Power* and *Foundations for the World's New Age of Plenty,* has made clear how essentially our systems of money and credit are part of our property and profit mechanism. One cannot use profit as the principle to get production and its opposite, the social dividend, to get distribution. No money scheme can make a fundamental change in the class ratio of distribution which assigns rich rewards to property owners and maintenance to workers. Logically, the money system is part of the property system. Hence the production of new goods is attended under our system by the production of new debts to those who advanced the credit which essentially is a social creation. Socially, credit is the right of workers to live on what has been produced, while they produce something more. But this is today a property right of finance capital, a right often attacked by other property owners who resent its claims, but essentially part of the property system. It is the whole point of this book that it is the disintegration of the capitalist system and not of the monetary system, which is the root of our disease.

Simply as an immediate palliative, especially in a capitalist society which will not face the capital levy without nervous collapse, I have always preferred reflation or controlled and directed inflation to a continuance of such deflation as marked the Hoover Administration. The gold standard is a fetish which we ought to outgrow, but because it is a fetish generally accepted I suppose we shall have to make some use of it for a while longer, especially for international exchange in a world where nations are of such different economic culture and there is as yet no economic international control. Ultimate stabilization on the basis of the devalued gold dollar and the English pound is probably the goal the present Administration should seek, if for no other reason because of the dangers to peace in wars between currencies. On the road to such a goal various devices could be used to check an inflationist orgy. Among them should be an agreement not to print paper money to pay the ordinary expenses of government, but I have never been able to understand why the entire expense of useful public works, many of them self-liquidating and all of them additions to real wealth, should be paid out of money derived from the sale of interest-bearing bonds. Why should not some form of treasury notes be used, limited in amount to a sum which will not force the price level out of hand, and with careful provisions for their retirement? The benefits of this controlled inflation would primarily accrue to workers and be specifically directed to reëmployment. Workers can be protected by a plan which I have been urging ever since the codes began and to which I have previously referred in this book, under which wages would automatically rise with the price of living. Finally, it is to be observed that any real control of money, including bank credit for social ends, requires the socialization of banking. A properly conducted, nationally owned and controlled banking system would have prevented the extremes of inflation and deflation which we have suffered. The great profits which now go to bankers who first buy bonds on which they get interest and then use these bonds as reserves against which to lend money—really to create money and credit—at further profit to themselves would be diverted to the public if the public owned the banks. No particular theory for achieving a commodity dollar and no type of controlled inflation will enable Mr. Roosevelt to do what he might have done by a proper nationalization of banks.

If monetary inflation gets out of hand it will give our economic system no strength but the strength of fever. The stimulus to industry will not equal in value to workers the lag in their salaries or wages. A large part of the middle class will be wiped out and, when the orgy is over and we are reëstablished we shall not have abolished an owning class but only changed its composition. We shall not have ended capitalism but only entered another phase of its disintegration. We shall not have ended the burden of debt but only capriciously lightened it to start the dance of debt and production anew. If wholesale inflation should prove to be the next step in the New Deal its effects will completely overshadow everything else the New Deal has tried to do and make it relatively unimportant.[1]

This is one reason why I suspect Mr. Roosevelt and his closest advisers will put up considerable resistance

[1] Since this chapter was in type Mr. Roosevelt has put through legislation for a managed currency on the basis of a dollar devalued in terms of gold to between fifty and sixty cents plus a stabilization fund for the treasury department to play with. I attempt no detailed

to wholesale inflation. Mr. Roosevelt does not want his other schemes completely wiped out or completely overshadowed. He will scarcely be content merely to tinker with money. He will do more than that. There is a considerable school of Mr. Roosevelt's admirers, some of them men who hold responsible offices under the New Deal, who openly proclaim or more subtly intimate that we must expect what they call a move of the Administration to the left. Mr. Roosevelt, they tell us, is quietly laying or has already begun to lay the foundation for much more thoroughgoing social control of banking, of the use of farm lands, and in particular of patents and inventions to prevent the nullification of his New Deal by technological unemployment. Some of them go as far as to say that politically he will, if necessary, smash his own party to bring about a new political alignment. One of his most stalwart newspaper supporters, Mr. Drew Pearson, capped the climax by telling an audience that Mr. Roosevelt was as radical as Mr. Scott Nearing and myself and then adding that if the country were to go Fascist, Mr. Roosevelt would still be on top!

---

criticism of the measure. It is certainly good that the Administration will take for the nation the immense profits of this devaluation of gold. I do not believe the law will satisfy the demand for inflation unless it results in a more dangerous degree of inflation than seems immediately likely. The exorbitant demands of the silver men will continue. The debt problem will remain. Perhaps the President's summary dealing with the so-called property rights of the holders of gold and the cancellation of the gold clause in bonds has set a precedent for dealing with creditors and property owners which Socialists can extend.

All this we can judge better when we have discussed the present condition of social forces in America. They have a way of being stronger than the strongest man. The definite slowing up, as I write, either of the Administration's ability or of its desire or of both, to get conditions favorable to labor and to labor organization, does not argue any great shift to the left. Certainly General Johnson's declaration to the A. F. of L. Convention that Labor should abolish the right to strike and accept government supervision of unions, is not evidence of any move to the left, unless one perversely regards Fascism as to the left. At any rate, we have clearly come to a time when the Roosevelt revolution, if it is to be any sort of revolution at all, will have to adopt consciously some sort of philosophy. It cannot continue as a grand adventure in opportunism, an adventure which is to make everybody happy. Indeed it never has been as experimentally detached from underlying philosophies as some of its admirers supposed. By every important test the Roosevelt program, with the possible exception of the Tennessee Valley Authority, is, as we have seen, a program of state capitalism.

It is likewise and appropriately a program of economic nationalism. It could hardly be otherwise in our sort of world. Mr. Roosevelt's apparent hope in April and May that he could go in for economic internationalism at the London Economic Conference and some old-line Democratic business of reducing tariffs, while at the same time he was working for a national control of agriculture, industry, and price levels was self-contradictory. No one, Republican, Democrat, Socialist, or Communist, can marry a planned national economy to a more or less *laissez-faire,* free trade international economy. The internationalism upon which ultimately peace and prosperity depend, must be an internationalism in which there is a steadily increasing world-wide control of working conditions, allocation of raw materials and currency. But for this those protagonists of conflicting views in the early stages of the Roosevelt Administration, the old-line Democrat, Cordell Hull, Secretary of State, and the college professor, Raymond Moley, Under-Secretary of State, but chief of the Brain Trust, were equally unprepared. In the end, Mr. Hull kept his job and Mr. Moley didn't, but Mr. Moley's point of view won. Mr. Roosevelt condemned the London Conference, which he had once professed to love, to utter futility and ultimate death by a cable sent with symbolic appropriateness from the battle. cruiser *Indianapolis*. The cable was a more extreme expression of economic nationalism than the statement which Mr. Moley had approved in London. It probably was politically shrewd in its effect on American public opinion at the moment, but it committed us to a rampant economic nationalism, the end of which no man can see. Part of the beginning of this heightened nationalism was the immediate diversion from the appropriation for public works of $128,000,000, to build the Navy up to full treaty strength. Apologists for this say that we had to do it to keep up with Japan and Great Britain. They say the same of us. And a hungry world goes on pouring its money into the bottomless pit of military preparation. Already the Roosevelt Army and Navy Budget has reached the highest point ever reached by the United States, save in 1916 when the whole world was in flames. These are bad omens, not cancelled by such common-sense diplomacy as the belated recognition of Russia, patience toward revolutionary Cuba, and fair words about disarmament and peace.[1]

It would be unfair to blame Mr. Roosevelt or the American people for seeking some control of its own economic life as the thing most immediately possible. Although such control is inconsistent with *laissez-faire* internationalism, it was not consistent with the use of the London Conference, at least to prepare the way for some eventual stabilization of currencies and for a modification of a tariff system which has less to do with scientific control of any nation's economic life than with the greed and short-sightedness of powerful spe-

---

[1] By the end of January, the single most alarming trend of the Administration was its big navy problem. Its militaristic tendency was emphasized by an amazing eulogy of the army as the means of preserving social order, "a nation within a nation," which had shown what it could do in the case of the Civilian Conservation Corps, and was more than willing to take over most of the new bureaus Mr. Roosevelt had set up—all this by no less a person than the Assistant Secretary of War, Mr. Woodring, former governor of Kansas. (See *Liberty,* Jan. 6.)

cial interests within each nation. We do live in an interdependent world, and no matter how persuasively it may be presented to us, the economics of autarchy or economic nationalism is in the long run the economics of Fascism and not the economics of either prosperity or peace. Our absorption in our domestic affairs must not blind us to this aspect of the New Deal. It is just now less imperialistic than some of its predecessors, chiefly because the times are not auspicious to aggressive imperialism in a world where imperialism has not recently paid dividends. But wars of tariffs and currencies in the name of the national autocracy may be just as dangerous to peace as the older imperialism and they are likely to lead, if we escape an immediate collapse of the capitalist system, into new expressions of imperialism, new struggles for markets, for places to invest, and new sources of supply for those raw materials which the strongest nations cannot find in sufficient quantities in their own borders. History may yet record that the nationalism implicit in the New Deal was as disastrous to America as was the capitalism to which it was allied, and that for the increase of this national emotion the workers paid a price out of all proportion to such benefits as they reaped from the reformist idealism which tried to change capitalism but not to build the coöperative commonwealth.

CHAPTER VII

SOCIAL FORCES IN AMERICA

IT remains to be seen how profound is the effect of the depression and the "Roosevelt Revolution" upon American thinking and American institutions. Some things, however, are clear. The course of events has immensely damaged the prestige of bankers and great industrialists who used to rank in the Coolidge epoch as prophets and kings on earth. At the time when bank failures were the order of the day, bankers became the subject of ribald jests even in Rotary and Kiwanis clubs. It would be a mistake, however, to infer from this that the dominant sentiment of America has definitely swung away from the profit system. Middle-class sentiment— and middle-class sentiment is still dominant sentiment— is willing to listen to a great deal that it once regarded as heresy. A lot of illusions and delusions have been swept away in the wreckage of the last few years, but popular wrath is still directed against certain specific failures of the profit system rather than the system itself, and many a man whose vigorous denunciation of things as they are makes him sound like a Communist who talks the American vernacular, seeks in reality not the coöperative commonwealth of workers but a return to the days of Andrew Jackson plus the automobile and radio and bathtub.

It would be a mistake, therefore, to suppose that the economic and political power of our business interests is as seriously impaired as their tarnished prestige would indicate. "Who own the earth will rule it" is still a sound generalization, even if the owners of the earth have been forced to make some concessions to virtue and fair play on the well-known principle, "The devil was sick, the devil a monk would be." If they ever get well or think they are getting well, the rest of the couplet will be fulfilled before our eyes. Indeed, it is being fulfilled in the returning arrogance of the employing class and its cynical flouting of the codes.

What gives the producing masses a somewhat better chance is the marked disunity of business interests which the New Deal has created or accentuated. That was strikingly illustrated in the reception of Mr. Gerard Swope's plan for what was well called "business Fascism," that is, a government of industry, by big business, and for big business, through a chamber of commerce and industry with scarcely more than veto power reserved to the government. From the standpoint of great corporations this was the logical development of the codes. Fortunately for America, Mr. Swope propounded this scheme, which was in essence simply a revival of a plan which had won no great support in the

Hoover Administration, at the very moment when Mr. Pecora was debunking business heroes as few classes in history have ever been debunked. Mr. Swope's first version of his revised plan never so much as mentioned farmers and consumers—after all, they do exist in America—and made only incidental reference to labor. Still worse from his point of view, he had done so little or so ineffective missionary work among his business asociates that the president of the National Manufacturers' Association was among the first to denounce the plan.

It does not follow that business will split on the extension of government control after the emergency legislation lapses on the same lines as on the Swope Plan. The great split which is already begun, will be between those who accept state capitalism as inevitable, if capitalism is to arrest even temporarily its own disintegration, and those who want to turn the clock back. The former will win because the logic of events is on their side. But they will not win without a hard-fought battle or series of battles, in the course of which the present political alignment in America is likely to be changed. In short, the owning class at this stage of the disintegration of capitalism is still powerful, but it does not present a united front on any of the major features of the Roosevelt program from the codes to inflation. Of this fact, workers with hand and brain, if they are alert, will take advantage.

But to take advantage of the situation the workers must be better organized and more united. In the crisis Mr. Roosevelt was forced to act vigorously and, at first, in a way pleasing to labor, because of the gravity of the situation rather than because the workers were well organized, aggressive and competent, in urging a program of action. He found the American Federation of Labor at hand, which with all its weaknesses was stronger than anything else. It is rather surprising that his Administration and the more astute industrialists did not try to use it more openly. Its leaders hated Communism and distrusted Socialism rather more than they hated or distrusted Wall Street. They were made to order to play the rôle of fairly docile junior partners in a scheme of enlightened state capitalism. They welcomed section seven of the National Recovery Act, which permitted organization and required collective bargaining, as a drowning man might welcome a life line or a hungry man manna from Heaven. Some unions or their leaders, notably the United Mine Workers and certain of the needle trades, saw what was coming even before it arrived, and by pushing their organization put themselves in a position to bargain advantageously. (Even so, President Lewis of the United Mine Workers could not have got anything like the Appalachian Agreement for the soft coal miners, if some thirty thousand rebel miners with no affection for him or confidence in him had not forced the fighting.) There was enough vigor in the A. F. of L., with the encouragement of powerful groups within the Administration itself, to enable it to add 1,300,000 workers between its annual convention in the Fall of 1932 and the Fall of 1933. Besides this there was a great deal of spontaneous organization outside the A. F. of L. The Railway Transportation Brotherhoods, which had never been in the A. F. of L., had strength enough in their own right to force protective clauses for workers into the law for the coördination of railroads. Unquestionably in the first eight months of the Roosevelt Administration the workers won much. But it is noteworthy that even in the honeymoon days of Roosevelt's so-called partnership, no union either in or out of the A. F. of L. was able to make much progress in organizing such basic industries as automobiles, steel, and aluminum. For this a great part of the fault lay in the ideals and methods of the A. F. of L. unions. It would be incredible if it were not true that in all its years of life and in spite of all its high pretensions, the American Federation of Labor never developed a technique adequate to an age of factory production when craft lines had become almost meaningless. After the death of Samuel Gompers it had lost the unifying and driving force of his personality. It held its constituent unions together on the basis of a loose federation, something like the very unsatisfactory Confederation which united the thirteen states before the adoption of the Constitution. That its critics, especially its radical critics, had often made a serious mistake in fighting it from the outside instead of trying to build it into something better from within, did not alter or excuse the fact that neither before nor after the coming of the New Deal did the A. F. of L. develop the machinery or the ideal necessary to make it the efficient economic spokesman of the working class. In the black Winter of 1932-33 it developed no power and no program as the spokesman of workers employed and unemployed. Had there been no New Deal the A. F. of L. might have been swept along in the turbulent channels of popular unrest. It could not have canalized that unrest or directed its energies.

This statement of fact is not a plea to the workers to get rid of the American Federation of Labor—anything but. No realist who knows the difficulty of building a well-established union can lightly contemplate the scrapping of the imperfect unions we have. No realist who is aware of the hatred and confusion bred by dual unions and the immense advantage they give to a hostile owning class, can lightly contemplate years or even months of struggle between rival unions in the same fields. All he can say is that a dual union is better than no real union, or a union dominated by racketeers, or a union which exists because its leaders have been taken into junior partnership with the employers. The thing that must be done is to transform and strengthen the A. F. of L. The Socialist who suggests some of the more obvious measures to be taken must not be considered the foe of the A. F. of L. nor as one who desires to establish a dictatorship of a party over the labor union movement. They should work together in harmony. It is not the business of the Socialist or any other party to capture the A. F. of L. unions by hook or by crook. It is the business of Socialists in unions and in sympathetic relations with them to persuade them by fair and open means to those courses of action which may strengthen us all in a struggle against Fascism in America. Certainly it is the business of Socialists in labor unions to act like Socialists and not to act like Republicans and Democrats, a point which has on occasions been forgotten.

It is from this point of view, then, that I suggest something that must be done, and done quickly if the A. F. of L. is to be a vital force for the emancipation of the workers, not a more or less unwilling tool of certain groups of employers.

First, the A. F. of L. unions must organize on the industrial basis. There are very few trades or callings where craft unions can longer be effective. How can anyone fit blacksmiths, machinists and fifty-seven other varieties of craft unions into the General Motors without endless fights between them over jurisdiction and frequent situations when some unions will be striking and others breaking the strike? They must be amalgamated into industrial unions, and, in fields not already occupied by the unions, the principle of industrial unionism must be asserted from the beginning. Industrial unions can go wrong, as history has plainly shown. Craft unions can hardly go right when there are twenty or more in one factory. The New Deal has made it fashionable to talk not of craft or industrial unions but of horizontal or vertical unions. The new terms are less descriptive than the old, from a labor standpoint. A vertical union might be only a plant union controlled by the employers. A true industrial union must organize the whole automobile industry, not simply the Ford or Chrysler factories. The single most disquieting fact in labor developments in the Fall of 1933 was that the A. F. of L. Convention instead of going forward toward industrial unionism, on the whole, went backwards. It voted to order the Brewery Workers Union to surrender members to some of the craft unions which demanded them. In general, it reassured the heads of the craft unions who on the eve of the Convention had expressed their fear of the temporary plant unions which the Executive Council of the A. F. of L. had wisely allowed to grow up, and warned the A. F. of L. that they would demand their "property rights" in the membership dues of workers included in the plant unions. True, the A. F. of L. did not smash the plant unions and it left the way open for further negotiations. Yet the future is not very bright because there is so little time to lose if the A. F. of L. is to take its rightful place in organizing the unorganized, who must be organized along industrial lines.

The second vital necessity for effective unionism is the realization that workers collectively in organized unions share the responsibility for organizing the unorganized. They cannot calmly leave the struggle to the particular union in the field, to the Textile Workers, for instance, who are nearly overwhelmed with the magnitude of the task before them. The reasons for this are both practical and theoretical. Practically it is absurd to talk of organizing the unorganized in a country the size of the United States when there is no central machinery of strategy, of relief, or of legal defense. The A. F. of L. expects its soldiers in the front ranks of battle to be their own commissary department. At most A. F. of L. relief of strikes comes only through the slow process of appeal to individual unions to make donations to support their brothers. There is no permanent machinery of relief, no reserve fund for the support of strikes or organizing campaigns, except as the constituent unions of the A. F. of L. may be able to amass such funds for themselves. It is precisely in those fields where unionization is most necessary that the constituent unions of the A. F. of L. are weakest and have no reserve funds. Hence the importance of action by the A. F. of L. as a whole. This is true in the matter of relief; it is equally true in the matter of labor defense. Thousands of dollars are wasted yearly, quite unnecessarily, because the dearly bought experience of unions in legal battles is not made available to all unions and there is no central organization for legal aid corresponding to the International Labor Defense set up by the Communists. When we consider the moral effect upon the workers, the case for central action by the whole body of workers in an organizing campaign is even stronger. We have seen that one reason for the weakness of the German unions in the hour of crisis was that, imperceptibly to themselves under the German cartels and labor agreements, unions had become used to working with the employers in terms of the well-being of the industry. They were industry, rather than class, conscious. The danger is far greater in the United States. Lines between skilled and unskilled trades are even sharper; hence the need of insisting that organization is of vital concern to the whole mass of workers, and that there can be no islands of safety in an unorganized sea. In this all-important direction the A. F. of L. Convention in the crucial month of October, 1933, took no adequate action.

A third change in A. F. of L. laws and customs should be to make real within unions that democracy for which A. F. of L. leaders so loudly stand as against both Communists and Fascists. Actually few dictatorships could be more extreme than the power given in some unions to presidents, who can suspend members without a hearing and thus deprive them, under certain conditions, of a chance to work at their trades. One of the reasons for the discouraging growth of labor unions is the widely diffused feeling among workers that the unions themselves are new instruments of tyranny and exploitation. This feeling is often unfair and usually exaggerated, but there is some basis for it. In union after union the individual member has scarcely as sure protection in his right as a member, provided he falls out with the dominant faction, as he has as a citizen of the political state. And that is saying a great deal! Of course the extreme tyranny of unions over the members arises when racketeers capture the union. Against this evil President Green and others influential in the A. F. of L. have recently made some headway. But there has not yet been a movement to set up a labor court as a protection of the rights of individual members; in consequence there has been the growth of a dangerous tendency for workers to drag their union troubles into the civil courts, which not only reflects on the prestige of the unions in the eyes of workers, organized and unorganized, but lays the foundation for control over them by the capitalist state. The danger of capitalist control through the machinery of the state is increased tenfold when warring labor unions, let us say A. F. of L. and Communist, rush into court. There is at least one case on record of an A. F. of L. union, one with a Socialist background which it has dishonored, that actually went into the courts in collusion with the employers to fight a Communist-controlled union. This is to invite destruction. It is the very antithesis of true democracy.

Equally it is the antithesis of true democracy that such slow progress has been made in wiping out the color line in A. F. of L. unions. There are still a few unions which by rule, and more unions which by custom, discriminate grossly against Negroes, thereby inviting them to join the bosses and become strikebreakers or to go over to the Communists. Here again the A. F. of L. Convention in the critical month of October, 1933, took no constructive action. The pity of it is the greater because most Negroes had found that the N. R. A. functioned as a Negro Removal Act.

Finally it is the condition of effective labor action that the workers should have political organization of their own. It is not the business of the A. F. of L. to be a political party or to set up a puppet party to dance as it pulls the strings; it ought to be its business to declare for the necessity of independent working-class political action and to facilitate the proper organization of it.

In justice to the A. F. of L. and the facts of the situation it must be acknowledged that workers dissatisfied with existing unions did not flock to other unions to improve their situation. The Communist unions made slow headway when one considers the genuine devotion that has been poured into building them. The National

Miners Union, Communist in origin, won a victory in spite of an early attempt to invoke N. R. A. against it at Gallup, New Mexico, after a three months' struggle. Another significant Communist-controlled strike was the strike of migratory cotton pickers in California in the early Fall of 1933. It was a strike abundantly justified and very well led. Only a very tiny minority of the pickers could be called Communist in any true sense of the word but the Communists who had initiated organization proved themselves level-headed and courageous in the conduct of the strike. Too often Communist organizing campaigns have suggested a union so completely dominated by the party for ends outside the immediate concern of the workers that those who were being organized for a strike have been turned away from the Communist unions in bewilderment or disgust. More than once I have heard Communist speakers in critical labor situations insist on spending an hour on every issue under the sun from the glory of Soviet Russia to the need of protecting China from imperialism before getting down to brass tacks. The Communist system, on the motto dear to every fanatic, "He that is not for us is against us," has been divisive and disruptive on the labor field.

Independent unions neither A. F. of L. nor Communist, as I have already said, are springing up in considerable numbers in all parts of the country. Some of them are getting away to a promising start. The most encouraging sign on the labor horizon as I write is an amalgamation of several contending unions in the boot and shoe field into one strong, militant organization which may yet supersede the present A. F. of L. union, which is usually ineffective save as it is an ally for the employers. In Illinois there had once seemed to be a genuine rank and file idealism about the Progressive Miners of America. Alas, in their struggles with the United Mine Workers, they developed characteristics which scarcely distinguished the new organization from the old in method or ideals. Experience shows that mere opposition to, or revolt against, the A. F. of L. is not a guarantee of a higher type of unionism.

I have dwelt upon the labor union situation not because it is the weakest manifestation of the organized strength of the workers as producers and consumers, but because it is the strongest. No consumers' co-operatives, immensely valuable as that expression of power has proved itself in Europe, have made in America anything like as much progress as the labor unions. This absence of organized consumer strength made it perfectly natural that the weakest feature of the New Deal was the representation it gave to consumers and their interests. Recognition of this side of things in the Roosevelt program remained largely a formal affair, more or less on paper. It was only after most of the codes were signed that belatedly something was done to strengthen consumer organization and its voice in the

New Deal. This organization, of course, fell far short of actual creation of consumers' coöperatives. In many cases it is, now, too late to build them. It is in general more hopeful to plan to socialize the chain stores than to organize the coöperatives to compete with them. But such socialized chain stores will be the stronger if they can ultimately be turned over to operation by consumers' coöperatives.

It goes without saying that the early months of the New Deal saw no great growth of a working-class political party or parties. The first tendency was to wait and see how far to the left Mr. Roosevelt himself might move and how far he could carry his party with him. 1933 was an off year so far as elections were concerned. Such municipal and other elections as were held afforded Mr. Roosevelt rather more encouragement than either Socialists or Communists. Socialists lost ground in the New York City election largely because of the support given to that opportunistic radical or radical opportunist, Major LaGuardia, Fusion candidate for Mayor, against a disunited and discredited Tammany. On the other hand the Socialists won favorable notice by their decisive municipal victory in Bridgeport where, however, the issue was less Socialism than honest and capable administration in the interest of workers and home owners, to which latter class many of the workers belong. More significant for Socialism was the fact that in a special election in Arizona for Representative at Large, the Socialist party came in second, well ahead of the Republican.

All in all the political situation in America after nine months of the New Deal was an amazing comedy with dangerous possibilities of tragedy. The first vigorous and open attack upon certain features of the "Roosevelt Revolution" came not from the Republican Party but from William Randolph Hearst who had supported Mr. Roosevelt in 1932, and, on other grounds, from none other than Alfred Emanuel Smith himself. Whatever the New Deal has or has not accomplished, it certainly has not revolutionized the Democratic Party. Democratic state governments swept into office by the Roosevelt tidal wave have shown no glimmer of New Deal idealism. They proceeded along the old lines, often proving more reactionary, perhaps out of inexperience, than their Republican predecessors. There was so little sense of cohesion or direction in the Democratic Party that when Tammany Hall was at last forced by the desperate needs of the unemployed to propose an essentially sound tax on stock market transactions, its officials were bludgeoned into submission by the brokers and bankers of New York with the cheerful coöperation of the Democratic authorities of New Jersey. The latter gentry not only welcomed but invited the stock market to move to Newark or to Jersey City and assured it that it would be free from the burdens of taxation. Mr. Roosevelt, the national leader, kept still; he did not even announce that he would propose to the next Congress a national tax on stock transactions which the New York markets could not so easily escape. Perhaps he was held back by some respect for the states' rights about which he used to talk before his election. So far as states' rights go, he has proved once more that the best way to bring about a strong and effective central government is to elect a Democrat. Like his Democratic predecessors, Cleveland and Wilson, he has done more to bring forward the powers of the Federal Government than any Republican. Yet most of his party go on mumbling about states' rights and Jeffersonian principles, even at a time when, as some cynics observed, about the only states' right that is left is the right to lynch. However one looks at it, the New Deal remains Roosevelt's revolution, not his party's. If there is any doubt in the matter imagine what would happen should the Vice-President—his name is Garner, in case you have forgotten—succeed to office!

The Republican Party is, if possible, even more divided. The gulf between LaFollette, George Norris, and the Western progressives, on the one hand, and Ogden Mills and Herbert Hoover, on the other, is wider and deeper. The national machinery of the party is in the hands of the Mills-Hoover group. If it has any program other than a program of negatives no one knows what it is. Its only strategy is to win by taking advantage of its opponent's mistakes.

Mr. Roosevelt has proved that in a crisis a strong man can do something in a confused political situation of this sort. Doubtless he still believes that he can have his way by an illogical and shifting series of coalitions between his more or less loyal Democratic followers and progressive Republicans, and carry his more important measures. It is not dictatorship, but it is personal government carried to the nth degree, a dangerous form of personal government because in it is no such security of permanence as party government at its best; that is when a party has some philosophy and program to carry out. As we have seen there are among the President's admirers those that think that he stands ready to bring forth a new political alignment. Others believe that he can prevail without it. Probably he will get enough to satisfy himself and not take the risk of kicking over the traces. Were he to form a New Deal Party it would probably be to the left of his present Administration, but there is no evidence that it would be consciously a party of workers with hand and brain looking toward a coöperative commonwealth.

That field is still left to the Socialist and Communist parties. The Socialist Labor Party persists as a sect with no political significance. None of the other minor parties which ran tickets in a few states in 1932 is likely in its present form to do more than survive—if that. There is a growing volume of talk about an independent Farmer-Labor Party. Conceivably circumstances may precipitate sentiment for such a party in definite and hopeful shape within the next few months. What those circumstances may be and what the conditions under which Socialists might find a mass labor party more effective for progress toward the coöperative commonwealth than the Socialist Party we shall be better able to discuss when we have completed our analysis of social forces and trends.

Certainly in classifying organized forces *now* operating not much space need be given to any radical political party outside the Socialist and Communist parties. Over Labor Day on the initiative of the League for Independent Political Action at a conference at the University of Chicago—rather academic setting that, for the embattled farmers and workers—a group of interesting persons of varied points of view but with no particular representative character, got together in the name of unity, and on the basis of rewriting the Socialist platform of 1932 started one more federation to form an inclusive Farmer-Labor Party. Then the delegates went their respective ways and nothing in particular has happened. As I write it seems at least as likely, if this federation lives at all, that it will be just one more of the little groups or sects into which the American radicals have a capacity amounting to genius for organizing themselves as that it will become a unifying force and the precursor of any genuine mass movement. Up to the present it is simply a statement of fact that if the individuals who have nothing more to propose than a version, often a watered-down version, of the Socialist platform, would have come into the Socialist Party and worked in it, we should all have been farther along. To which it may fairly be retorted that the Socialist Party itself is challenged to self-criticism in an effort to find out to what extent its own failures or shortcomings may be responsible for the failure of the growing number of those who largely share its philosophy and embrace its program to enter its ranks, to stay within them, and build the party up. Socialists are usually able to make a trenchant and logical criticism of those near-Socialists who do not join them and those individuals who, protesting their Socialist convictions, nevertheless leave the party in an effort, which in the past has always been unsuccessful, to get their cause ahead faster by some other political tactics. The plain truth is that these admirable criticisms win no battles. To prove that those who do not come with you or stay with you are wrong-headed may be an intellectual satisfaction, but it is poor compensation for failure to build the mighty movement which the times demand.

No wonder, then, that there is growing concern in radical circles about the need of the United Front in America. It is unfortunate that that particular descriptive phrase has acquired a somewhat narrow and technical meaning. It is applied to efforts to get Socialists and Communists together. To say that they ought to get together in the face of their common enemy, Fascism, is as true as to say that doctors should get together in the face of their common enemy, disease. But if doctors honestly disagree as to the treatment for the patient they can scarcely be asked to get together by drawing lots as to what to do. The disagreement between Socialists and Communists in method, tactics, psychology, is sharp, nowhere sharper than in the United States. What I have said in an earlier chapter about the impossibility of organic unity between Socialists and Communists admits of no American exception. Socialists do not put a mechanical vote-counting democracy ahead of Socialism, but they are not convinced that a dictatorship which has split Communists in America into at least three groups besides the official party can produce a workers' democracy. Socialists know that the change from a disintegrating capitalism to the coöperative commonwealth requires struggle. If a small handful of Socialists are Tolstoyan, most of them are fully aware that the working class cannot renounce all right to use of violence in the face of an owning class which uses it habitually. But Socialists intend to emphasize that there is effective struggle which falls short of the mass murder of civil war or terrorism, and they present Socialism as an alternative to widespread violence of this order, not its doubtful consequence. Responsible Communists do not love violence for its own sake. The American Communist Party is strong in its insistence that the time for insurrectionary violence in the United States lies in the indefinite future; nevertheless it insists upon the necessity of large-scale violence or rather its inevitability. It seems a little less sure than it used to be that World Revolution in its American phase must grow out of world war and that in the end the only road to peace is to turn foreign war into civil war. Yet it thinks that is probable. Thus, the Communist leader, M. Olgin, speaking at a peace meeting at Hunter College, New York, talked about the ultimate necessity of turning foreign war into civil war, which latter he said would be less devastating than foreign war! Of course the precise contrary is the case. Socialists are internationalists, certainly as against the devastating nationalism of Fascism, but all recent events strengthen their conviction that in every country each Socialist movement must have autonomy and its success depends upon adapting itself to conditions in the country and the predominant psychology of the country. The Communist's internationalism means a rigorous control from headquarters of the Third International in Moscow. It is a paradoxical fact that the Communist's internationalism is as successful as it is in controlling every Communist party simply because it is not a true internationalism. I have previously pointed out that the Third International is dominated by Russia, its policies are shaped on the basis of Russian needs and Russian conceptions of the world situation. We have seen the effects of this in Germany. It has not helped the party in America. Even the faithful have hard work changing their opinions, or what they thought were their opinions, overnight. It was hard enough for them to swallow Litvinoff's $5.50 banquet in New York followed by his visit to Mussolini, but Stalin's virtual overtures to the much-cursed League of Nations to support Russia against Japan almost choked the true believers. Worse than the struggles of the faithful always to believe that Stalin knows best has been the attempt to copy a Russian plan in a very different situation. Because Russia had granted cultural autonomy to regions populated by various linguistic or racial groups, American Communists had to declare for that dangerous and wholly unsocialistic thing, self-determination in the black belt; that is, a setting up of states or counties some of them ruled by colored and some by white folk! And this in the name of solidarity of the working class! No wonder that the kind of dictatorship, and foreign dictatorship at that, has split off repeatedly from the American Communist Party some of its most valuable leaders. Today some of the most searching criticisms of official Communism come from the followers of Trotsky and the followers of Jay Lovestone.

Lillian Symes in a recent article entitled "Blunder on the Left" makes this comment on certain Communist tactics: "If Socialism spoke with an exotic accent, metaphorically speaking, Communism scarcely spoke English at all. Its vocabulary was indeed a marvelous thing to contemplate. But this was not its only drawback. Another lay in the fact that it came wrapped in the garments of medieval religiosity that made the Society of Jesus a college Liberal Club in comparison. It was a church that operated under the thumb of a College of Cardinals four thousand miles away and, for a decade, while the Party itself was rent with schisms, heresy-hunts, charges and counter charges of treachery, while each gesture of Moscow attuned to the Russian situation was matched in miniature by a similar gesture here in New York, thousands of convinced radicals and potential recruits were turned away."

Nevertheless, although organic unity between Socialists and Communists is impossible there is theoretically no bar to common action on a great many points, including the defense of such rights as workers now have, and opposition to Fascism and the war which Communists must oppose even though they believe that sooner or later it is inevitable. I have already acknowledged that I belong to that minority of Socialists who believe that under certain circumstances and in the face of grave danger, coöperation is immensely desirable and by no means wholly impossible. I should favor making some try at it in America without waiting for the loosely knit Second International to act. But the average American liberal or intellectual who looks on from the sidelines cannot understand how difficult is this coöperation by reason of the nature of the Communist attack. No one would expect the Communists to renounce their own theories or their own organization in a united front movement, but one might expect them in meetings and in other activities connected with that united front, to follow a policy of reasonable fair play toward their allies. This has not been the Communist policy. They are under instructions from Moscow at one and the same time to try to stop a Fascist movement in America by the united front and to use it to ruin the Socialist Party. It is putting it mildly to say that never in the various times when I have participated, and gladly participated, in a certain degree of common action, let us say in labor defense, have I been able to proceed without being continually on guard against sabotage. To be sure the Communists are so convinced that they are right that, when they practice it, sabotage is not sabotage. I have known them deliberately to break up a labor union in the midst of a strike when they found that they could not control it, all the while protesting that they, and they only, were the friends of the workers. Earl Browder, the leader of the party in America, has written: "We can never win the workers to a united front struggle, which means winning them away from the Social Fascist influence, unless we meet thoroughly and explain sharply the basic differences between ourselves and them." *Social Fascist,* be it noted, is the ridiculously misleading term applied to Socialists by Communists.

Even this curious conception of a united front, with intent to ruin your allies, might be more easily tolerated and dealt with by Socialists were it not that the process of winning workers away from Socialist influence includes all manner of slander and falsehood. These are harsh words. There is a devotion of Communists to their cause and a kind of fanatic faith in truth, their truth, which is superior to fact and in whose service facts may be distorted, which lifts them above men of less devotion who use their methods. Nevertheless there are difficulties in the way of an effective united front even for particular activities when your presumptive allies are so fertile in abuse of you. My individual relations with many Communists are pleasant and my respect for them and their devotion is high, but it is a little hard to remember that respect when I read in the Communist Press—and do not forget that all Communist papers are official papers, absolutely under party control—that I am "a supporter of lynching," that I said I would "support war if it was on the eve of its outbreak," that I "stood by and laughed while the police beat up an unemployed worker at City Hall." These are only a few of the gratuitous lies and slanders hurled against me which are made up out of whole cloth or out of deliberate distortion of statements or facts. I am not the worst sufferer from this sort of thing. No individual is the worst sufferer. These lies and slanders are rather clumsy, and the net effect of them is not to make Communists but cynics out of workers. At the very least one might expect the Communist Party to see that if the end justifies the means, it should use the means of falsehood and slander more subtly and discreetly. They are, however, justified in using those means by the precept and practice of the great Lenin himself. There is a veteran of the old Socialist Revolutionary Party of Russia now living in America who had an interesting tale to tell of how Lenin met his protest against some Bolshevist misrepresentation by saying, "Well, you and we are enemies, are we not? Of course it would be nice if we could tell the truth and only the truth about our enemies but—" The uncompleted sentence was more eloquent than words.

I should like to argue what I suppose is the old-fashioned notion that no desirable coöperative commonwealth will ever be established, even after the elimination of capitalism, if workers have been habitually taught to use any weapons that may be necessary to discredit their enemies not only outside but inside their class. At best the Communist dictatorship in Russia, as Trotsky has been pointing out, tends to produce a bureaucracy independent of workers, with its own ends in view, as if it were a new class in the state. If such a bureaucracy has been trained in the use of anything to win, the outlook for social happiness is far from happy. I am here, however, concerned less about life under a Communist dictatorship than about the conditions which have made the united front for a particular object

so difficult in America and which have also seriously
retarded the growth of a sound American working-class
movement. It is no answer to what I have said to single
out cases where it can be charged that Socialists have
retorted to Communists in kind, or, professing a belief
in democracy, have not practiced it as they ought. That
is doubtless true. In America Socialists have not yet, like
Communists, made a virtue out of their misdeeds, or
deliberately repudiated good faith as only a "bourgeois
virtue."

What hope there is in America, and probably in
Europe, as I have already said lies in the pressure of
sheer necessity that Socialists and Communists act together in certain matters unless they wish to be
destroyed separately. In the Anti-War Congress and its
Continuation Committee the Communist attitude has
made a genuine united front less impossible than it
would appear from some of their declarations. Non-
Communist organizations have found it possible by dili-
gence and intelligence to maintain coöperation. Encouraged by this fact, Socialists might have adopted
tactics which would not have put them so much on the
defensive in the public mind with regard to joint action
and so would have avoided a situation in which the lead
appears, however erroneously, to remain with Communists.

The theoretical considerations which make organic
union between Socialists and Communists do not apply

to the labor union field. Here an inclusive union is theoretically possible and Communists might bring a vigor and energy to that union of immense advantage. It would be necessary for them, however, definitely to abandon the disruptive tactics they have sometimes used and the attempt to dictate union tactics by the party and for party advantage.

Outside of the main job of organization there is a great deal of confused public opinion in America which has the significance of a social force. There never was a time in our past when the interest in Socialist theory and Socialist program was so great. A very striking proof of this was given by the assembling of some three thousand delegates to a Continental Congress in May. The Socialist Party had taken the initiative in calling this convention together. It had a surprisingly representative character and a spontaneous enthusiasm in excess of any convention in recent years called under strictly Socialist auspices. Delegates were almost unanimous for carrying on somehow. There developed a real desire for a farmer-worker party, bigger than the Socialist Party but to include it. Most of the Socialists with reason thought it was at least premature to organize such a party. The Continental Congress was, however, continued. In spite of a certain lack of definiteness and of great financial handicaps, and the diverting excitements of the New Deal, the continuation group manifested a vitality from which something may yet come.

In any estimate of social forces in America and in any consideration of the weakness of Socialism one must remember that historically the place generally taken in western Europe by a Socialist or other Marxian or near Marxian movement was, in America, taken by an agrarian radicalism or populism which grew out of the soil. The reason for this was to be found in the very nature of the United States as a pioneer country which afforded to many generations of the discontented an escape to new land. Naturally, then, their protest was less against ownership and an owning class, as that term has come to be understood, than in European nations which had evolved out of feudalism into capitalism without ever wholly shaking the characteristics of the static feudal order. Indigenous American radicalism after the Civil War turned not against all ownership but against monopolies, trusts, and the finance capitalism which centered in Wall Street. It had a geographic or sectional quality. In the language of Marxism, American radicalism was *petit bourgeois.* Yet it had about it an atmosphere of its own, unlike anything in Europe. So strong was the middle class in a country which had never had a genuine feudalism or a great aristocratic tradition that the workers themselves were impregnated with middle-class ideology. So many were the opportunities of escape out of the traditional working class that the strong and ambitious man more or less reasonably thought that he had a better chance to stake out his own homestead or to rise in the industrial or economic or business world than to help his own class to rise.

This indigenous American radicalism in action was by no means in love with slow evolution. Its votaries wanted results, they were not afraid of violence, at least on a local scale. They used direct action in strikes, they used direct action to save the homes of farmers from foreclosure, yet they would have indignantly repudiated revolution in a Marxian sense. This radicalism was always appealing, and rightly so, to the older American tradition of liberty and independence. It was fulfilling the ideals of a revolution already achieved.

During the great depression this native American radicalism has almost unconsciously taken on a somewhat more Socialist tinge. It is yet to be seen whether or not it will work out an adequate philosophy for the times. Even in the palmy days of the frontier the old agrarian philosophy was not adequate for its own purposes. The proof of it is to be found in the fact that the characteristic American radicalism was populistic and primarily concerned with cheap money. Nevertheless most of the farmers after the Civil War voted the Republican ticket in spite of the fact that the Republican Party was largely controlled by big business interests. Farmers supported a high tariff policy consistently in face of the obvious advantages to them of low tariffs in a country with excess wheat and cotton and corn to sell. The Republican Party maintained its hold on the farmers partly by misleading propaganda and largely because it had been the party which had passed the Homestead Act and given free land to the pioneer. Moreover it was a party of "moral ideals." It had freed the slaves. By means of this historical record and under these shibboleths and slogans it held power in the affection of farmers long after its real devotion was to the mammon of unrighteousness in Wall Street. But by 1932 the farmers and city workers got together in a negative revolution. They united in voting against Hoover.

Whether they will stay together and on what terms may determine the future of America. An imported philosophy, program and vocabulary based either on European Fascism or European Socialism will scarcely unite them. Whoever wins will have to talk the American language, but essentially the propaganda of unity will, in a broad sense, be either Fascist or Socialist.

Before we turn to the question which, there is something more to be said about American public opinion, this time in reference to peace. Nowhere have peace societies been more active and nowhere more futile. Unquestionably there has been genuine idealism behind the American desire for peace. But it has not been a very intelligent idealism and it has been unwilling to pay the price of peace. Generally speaking peace societies supported Wilson in the War and the League of

Nations after the War. Then they went rushing off in devotion to one panacea after another, always panaceas that would not cost too much in terms of the renunciation of personal, class or national profit and prestige. There was a stubborn refusal to recognize the fact that the very foundations of our capitalist nationalist society were the foundations of a warlike, not a peaceful, world. He who warned these pacifists that the price of peace was high and that organization for peace must go deep, was a voice crying in the wilderness; he was a "pessimist," he was blocking immediate action! Let us not worry, said they, about ultimates but support arbitration, disarmament, referendum before war, World Court, the outlawry of war, or even the generally unpopular League of Nations! Pacifist societies and most pacifist individuals declared a moratorium on their international principles every four years in order that they might vote Republican or Democrat according to their prejudices. Few of them made the recognition of Russia a cardinal point in their program of peace and plenty, and when belated recognition came it was the result of the operation of the desire for trade or the need of recognizing Russia in opposition to Japan which prevailed. These peace societies and pacifists either waxed sentimental over war debts and wanted to forgive them out of hand or else insisted upon their payment. There was almost no recognition of what might have been done by proper handling of the issue of war debts to promote a quiet revision of the most objectionable features of the Treaty of Versailles and disarmament. The relation of tariffs and other economic questions to peace remained for most pacifists an academic question: Why bother when one dose of the League of Nations or two of the World Court might do the trick? The desperate urgency of changing the system which is the breeder of war and at the same time preventing the outbreak of particular war was not understood. Yet the number of these pacifists or near pacifists and the existence of a public which is more persuaded than formerly of the cruelty and futility of war give one a modest hope that there is material which with proper organization and leadership might be used in a struggle for peace. If drift in America, as in the rest of the world, is toward war rather than peace it is not a drift without some counter current and without some possibility that men who dare may yet find their way of escape.

CHAPTER VIII

THE ROAD BEFORE US

THERE is no destiny which determines man's fate utterly without his power to dream and act. We ourselves help to make our fate. The forms of social organization are not absolutely and rigidly predetermined by forces outside of the generation which finds itself caught between the crumbling of the old and the coming of the new. Choice is not wholly illusory. But the field in which men may choose is limited. We shall not choose to smash our tools and begin over again. We shall not choose to revive a pastoral civilization. No nostalgia for Gothic churches and the color of the Middle Ages will take us back to a genuine medievalism, nor can Americans ever again enjoy in their own country the receding frontier which so powerfully shaped their earlier destiny. If our analysis has been correct we ought at this point to decide what roads are open to us and where they are likely to lead. On the basis of that decision our choice may better be made.

The road some men seek leads back to the older capitalism. Those who want to explore that road differ

162

widely as to the particular stage of the older capitalism
to which they would return. In practice they will probably settle on a repeal of the Roosevelt legislation. But
they will not wipe the slate clean again of Roosevelt's
laws. If they did, it would be no road back. The
processes of disintegration have gone too far. Suppose
all the New Deal legislation were to expire or to be
repealed. We should still have its consequences upon
us and added to them the consequence of the intervention of government in Hoover's time of which the Reconstruction Finance Corporation was the outstanding
instrumentality. We should still have the record, moreover, of the piracy and highway robbery which characterized the rule of big business. Now it is easy to fool
the people part of the time. Hitler has commented cynically on the possibility of misleading people by propaganda, but you can't forever fool the people by the
same propaganda, especially after it has been discredited. The myths which justified and supported the
Coolidge epoch have been made ridiculous in the eyes
of the masses. If they are to be cowed and kept in some
sort of subjection it must be by new myths, new illusions, new fears, new hopes, however false. We shall
not go backward. If in the unlikely event of temporary
victory a political party should simply attempt to go
backward the consequence would be disastrous.

The second theoretical possibility is for the extension
and stabilization of the Roosevelt New Deal. Those

who hope for this are, as we have seen, reluctant to give us a philosophy. Instead they rather exult in pragmatism of an opportunistic sort. They will increase social control, they will protect the underdog, they will stabilize business, and yet somehow or other preserve individual initiative, private profit, and the rights of the little man. Theirs will be an American plan, a capitalist collectivism without ruthless intolerance. I suspect that this or something like this is the Roosevelt ideal. Mr. Roosevelt is no Fascist and, unlike Mr. Pearson, I doubt if he could become the American equivalent of Mussolini. Your Fascist leader will have a different accent from Mr. Roosevelt's. He will be one of the masses, more familiar by experience with poverty, thwarted desires and frustrated ambitions than Mr. Roosevelt, who in the best sense of the word is an aristocrat. His one-time supporter and his present bitter enemy, Huey Long, would more nearly be the Fascist type, though Huey himself is not the man, especially since he lost the battle of the Long Island washroom. Mr. Roosevelt may have helped to unloose forces which will lead to Fascism but his success lies in the success of his own New Deal without Fascism. Moreover that success must be rapid. He has not given masses of the people any fanatic faith to sustain them or any new philosophy to guide them in a wilderness. He has promised results. His liberal aspirations are meaningless except as he gets results. It will not be enough that the New Deal should escape fresh economic disaster in the months that lie ahead. At the very least it must reduce unemployment to what was once regarded as a normal level, stop the almost universal "chiselling," and begin to raise the real income of the average farmer, worker and little man generally. Even if it begins to do this far more effectively than seems probable as I write, it will not be out of danger. A mild success of the New Deal on its own terms raises insistent questions. Why should the workers be content with so little if it is not the individual initiative of great capitalists but the fostering care of government which protects profit, rent and interest? Now to avoid that question or to divert the minds of the questioners will require stronger medicine emotionally than any talk about the New Deal, or "partnership," or the virtue of neighborliness. It will take something like the heady wine of Fascist nationalism to evade this insistent economic issue. That is why the road which the New Deal has opened will not reach any distant horizon without sharp detours to the right or the left.

There remain three possible or probable roads before us. One leads to catastrophe, arising from economic breakdown, or more probably new world war; another leads to some form of Fascism; a third to some form of Socialism. Perhaps my figure of speech is a bit misleading. What stretch out before us are not well-made roads but directions in which we can make our road. There are kinds and degrees of catastrophe. There may be more than one form of Fascism. There is certainly more than one form of Socialism if one uses it in a broad sense to include Communism.

Let us consider first the possibility of catastrophe. We were not far from such catastrophe arising from economic breakdown in the early months of 1933. The continuation of the conditions at the close of the Hoover Administration without countervailing forces would have meant catastrophe in our closely knit economic civilization. Such catastrophe may arise again out of wild and uncontrolled inflation, out of paralyzing deflation, out of complete breakdown of our system of banking and credit, out of the steady growth of unemployment without the stabilizing effect of social insurance, which we have not yet set up. Economic *catastrophe,* however, is unlikely. The chances are that we shall die a more lingering death, if only economic forces are operative and there is no new war.

The great danger of catastrophe in the near future arises from the possibility of the outbreak of world war which will draw America in. The whole point of the analysis we have been making is that such war is more likely than peace. There is no program, much less any panacea, to make peace sure during the next decade in Europe or in Asia. There are things worth doing to promote international economic agreements about currency, tariffs and debts. Disarmament has its values although it is by no means a guarantee of peace. The cause of disarmament, black as its outlook is today, is perhaps not altogether hopeless if by processes of evolution or revolution Fascist jingoism is checked. For the present President Roosevelt's proposals that no nation send troops across another's borders and that new offensive armament be stopped and what exists reduced have some value. Governments are likely to be more impressed by the fear of the general effect of war upon the masses and by the danger that new war will invite domestic revolt. Another aid to peace is Hitler's inability to acquire heavy arms in a hurry. There is, moreover, a chance that a popular, unofficial boycott, particularly if it would work to check the flow of certain goods into Germany as well as the purchase of goods from Germany, might have a salutary effect and economically lessen German ability to rearm on a large scale. Unless the boycott, dear to many Jewish and labor union enemies of Hitlerism, can be deliberately and carefully used, it may degenerate into a mere provocative of war. Any moral effect of a boycott by Americans against Germany will be lost unless we can stop our lynchings and racial discriminations.

There are some protections not to be despised against the spread of European war to the whole world. The British Empire has everything to lose from fresh world war and the sentiment of the English people for peace is probably stronger and more intelligent than that of

any other nation. Their relatively pacific attitude in
the face of De Valera's plans for an Irish Republic with
only very shadowy connections with the Empire or British Commonwealth is an encouraging sign which our
fathers would never have believed possible. More important is the declaration of the British Labor Party
against voting war budgets and for a general strike in
the event of war mobilization. That one of its major
parties has even seriously suggested this tends to make
Great Britain a barrier of some importance against the
spread of European war. It does not, however, guarantee perfect wisdom in handling the menace of Hitlerism in a way that will make for peace, not war!

Another aid to peace is the pacific policy followed by
Soviet Russia. This policy has even extended to the
relations between Soviet Russia and Japan although by
all ordinary standards the Russian position in Asia, as
well as Russia's particular rights in Manchuria, has
been definitely menaced by the advance of Japanese
imperialism. It is not likely that this extreme pacific
policy will continue indefinitely; already it is reported
that the Soviet Government is offering special induce-
ments to encourage the rapid colonization or upbuild-
ing of Siberia and the Manchurian border. Stalin has
publicly warned of the Japanese menace to peace. The
Russian attitude of forbearance may still further be
changed when the Trans-Siberian Railroad is double-
tracked. Yet it is reasonably certain that not Russia but

the Japanese imperialists will be the aggressors if war breaks out in the Far East.

The basis of Russia's pacific policy is twofold. First, the recognition of the necessity of building up Russia internally; and second, a genuine repudiation of the imperialist standards and aims of capitalist nations. Russia's rulers in their hearts doubtless desire to see the red flag flying over Constantinople, now Istanbul. The old urge to annex it to Russia as an outlet for Russia is done for. There is no special class of exploiters to seek profits in imperialism. Yet I cannot be as sure as some of the eulogists of Russia's pacific policy that Russia will never fight unless a direct attack is made against her. That is not quite in accord with even Stalin's version of world revolution. Moreover it is not in accord with the high degree of military preparedness in Russia and of military teaching in the schools. I grant that the Red Army has been trained as no other army in the world to be of use in time of peace as well as of war. I grant the original justification for it in the hostility of the capitalist West toward struggling Russia.

Nevertheless militarism is militarism, and the dogmatic teaching of inevitable war of capitalism against Communism will make it very easy for rulers less wise and possibly less moderate than those now in power to lead forth their hosts in a kind of offensive which is the best defensive. Napoleon consecrated some of his most imperialistic victories in the name of the revolution.

Russia has as yet produced no Napoleon. Her mind is set on economic victory, but she has her own regimentation. Does not Max Eastman's *Artists in Uniform* suggest an internal situation in which a ruling bureaucracy, out of mistaken fanaticism or some even less desirable quality, might easily order the regimented masses into war?

Against such a possibility the best defense is a policy of recognition of Russia and the inclusion of Russia on all possible occasions in every plan for disarmament and peace. The more obvious it can be made in the eyes of the world that there is not a capitalist unity against Russia, and that the class struggle does not mean inevitable world war, the greater is the assurance of peace. We have substantial foundations on which to build. Russian diplomacy has taken the lead in asking disarmament that is real. If this was only a bluff, at least the capitalist nations were thrown into a panic too great even to call the bluff. Only a few weeks ago at the International Press Congress, at Madrid, held under the auspices of the League of Nations, it was Russian delegates who introduced a resolution to stop armament manufacturers from giving subsidies to newspapers. This entirely reasonable and entirely necessary proposal for the protection of the people against wars fomented by journalists in the payment of those who profit by war and the preparation for war was defeated by the French delegates supported by their colleagues from

Little Entente countries. They dared not go home, they said, with such a proposal. It would mean the defeat of all else they had done! The story needs no comment as an illustration first, of the immense dangers to peace arising out of profits in armaments, and second, of the intelligent stand which the Russian delegates, in this case supported by Americans and others, took in a matter of primary importance.

The moral of the situation is that there is nothing in the position of Russia today in relation to the rest of the world which makes war inevitable. It is improbable that Hitler will succeed in persuading western Europe to grant him leadership and arms as the defender of capitalist nationalism from Communism. Already the capitalist system has too far disintegrated and the rivalries of capitalist nations are too great to make this degree of unity at all likely. The immediate probabilities of war do not arise from premeditated European attack on Russia or a Russian attack on her European neighbors. Into that kind of war the nations might stumble and fall if some half-mad dictator should throw a torch into that section of the powder magazine which a world in arms must always be. If, however, Russia is soon to be involved in war it will probably be in the Far East. In any war between Russia and Japan it is doubtful whether any capitalist solidarity would unite effectively the United States and other Western nations with Japan, in face of popular feeling and real or alleged national interests. It is significant that the moment of President Roosevelt's recognition of Russia seems to have been determined by the movement of Japanese troops on the Siberian border. What the President did was to make war less, not more, likely by a prompt recognition of Russia.

For America, Japanese imperialism is unquestionably one of the danger spots. It will not become less dangerous for our peace if we build up to treaty limits and then demand an extension of those limits for our navy. The truth is that neither the United States nor Japan could make an effective attack on the coast of the other. The less our military preparations are of the sort which would support aggressive war the less is the danger of war. The chief result of our big navy policy has not been to make us safer but to provoke suspicion, fear and rivalry, not alone in Japan, but in Great Britain.

There is no denying that Japan presents an immense problem to world peace. Nowhere, not even in Fascist Italy or Germany, does a mystical, almost insane, nationalism run more rampant. To assassinate men guilty of the most moderate opposition to the dreams of the militarists has become a patriotic virtue. The world-wide condemnation of Japanese occupation of Manchuria and her attack upon Shanghai were without effect. Perhaps if the world had been so organized that the nations in the League, with the addition of Russia and the United States, could have united promptly in an embargo against loans and the supply of material of war to Japan, something might have been done. This embargo would have fallen short of a complete economic boycott, which if it could be enforced against any nation might have many of the evil effects of war and rapidly lead to war. In any case it is now too late to use any such economic pressure unless against new acts of aggression. It is the old story. Once more we are faced with accomplished facts. Japan has maneuvered herself into a position where she has aroused ill will and suspicion in Russia and bitter and implacable wrath in China; a growing measure of hostility in her old ally Great Britain by her trade rivalry—not always, according to the British, carried on fairly; and enhanced popular distrust of her in the United States. As always happens in such cases the stronger her potential enemies the greater her sense of national righteousness. Under these circumstances the principles which guide American diplomacy ought to be three:

1. We should make it perfectly apparent to the world, and most of all to Japan and China, that we shall assume no rôle of St. George against the dragon on behalf of China. It would inevitably prove a hypocritical rôle. Were we under any conceivable circumstances to drive Japan out of Manchuria the chances are a hundred to one that we should then stay in Manchuria in order to civilize it. We should repeat on a larger and worse

scale the story of the Spanish War. In the long run China can take far better care of herself than if she seeks the dubious aid of Western imperialism against Japanese imperialism. The best help we could give to China would be to try quietly and persuasively to bring about a general conference on the Far Eastern situation, which conference would only succeed on a basis of a willingness of all powers, not merely Japan, to give up imperial rights in China.

2. In Latin America we can practice the doctrine we have so loudly preached to Japan. In terms of *real Politik,* that is, of extreme nationalistic interest, the Japanese militarists have far more justification for what they have done in Manchuria than we have had for our various versions of dollar diplomacy in Latin America. There is considerable justification for the Japanese attitude: "When we have caught up to you in stealing we will then join you in virtue." The mood and practice of the United States is now far less aggressively imperialistic than it was a few years ago. Popular resentment at the failure of certain Latin American states to meet their financial obligations, most of them held in this country, is fortunately and properly directed against the bankers who marketed these unsound loans rather than against the countries in question. The Marine Corps is enjoying a vacation from its accustomed missionary work in behalf of civilization, bankers, oil speculators and others. How long this vacation will last is

another matter. The world might be surer of us if we should promptly denounce the Platt Amendment, to which must be attributed in no small degree the miserable political condition in Cuba. The tyrant Machado, it must be remembered, was from the first a representative of American industry. Then we should get our Marines out of Haiti, and in all Latin America cultivate in reality a Pan-Americanism which heretofore has been sentimental and occasional. Such a policy as this would have immense advantages for other reasons than its possible effect upon Japan.

3. The final thing that we should do is to reassure Japan on certain specific issues. It is an incredible folly that we should continue to exasperate a proud nation by our contemptuous act of Japanese exclusion. One may grant that the world is not yet ready to permit unrestricted immigration between peoples so different as the Americans and Japanese, without admitting that it is necessary to insult the Japanese. Every necessary control of Japanese immigration could be exercised either by putting Japan under the quota law which applies to immigration in general, or still better by negotiating a bi-lateral treaty under which the United States and Japan mutually agree that nationals of one country (with certain carefully stated exceptions) will not emigrate to the other.

It might also minimize the possible danger of conflict with Japan were we to grant the Philippines their independence and to negotiate a general agreement among powers with Far Eastern possessions to guarantee the neutrality of the Islands. This is not a policy of abandoning the Philippines to the Japanese. Immediate neutrality would give the Philippines at least as good protection as we can give. Military and naval authorities agree that we cannot defend the Philippines against Japan in case of attack. We could only win them back again as part of the price of peace at the end of a long war. The Islands are not worth it to us, and if they were we ought not to hold them. They want their independence, they should be given it, and on terms which do not threaten them with economic ruin for the sake of our beet-sugar growing or other highly protected interests.

This cursory examination of some outstanding problems and possibilities ought to convince us that there is a program of immediate political action with regard to them which is worth trying. We have lost precious opportunities. We can do less with a program of immediate action than we might have done with a wise program at any time prior to the Japanese occupation of Manchuria and the victory of the Nazis in Germany. There never were any panaceas, but measures that seemed to promise some things, let us say in 1926, promise less today. There is a pathetic note about the occasional feeble voice raised to insist that the United States ought to join the League of Nations in the inter-

ests of peace at the time when the whole future of the
League is clouded with doubt. Nevertheless the extreme critics of the League ought to remember that its
present weakness grows out of its comparative virtue
rather than out of its essential inadequacy. The latter
is largely due to the nations which compose the League
and their unwillingness to surrender real powers to any
supra-national authority. The League did finally speak
the truth in its verdict on Japanese imperialism. It was
more friendly to disarmament, when real disarmament
was more likely than it has become since the Hitler
triumph, than was any one of the larger nations which
dominated it. Certainly the League's record is far better
than the record of France. The actual dissolution of
the League or its degeneration to extreme impotence
would be a definite loss because, however fine might be
an ideal substitute for the League, that would not come
into being on its death. Instead rampant nationalism
would more completely dominate the scene. Nevertheless American lovers of peace will be well advised not
to put so much emphasis on the League as certain right-
wing Socialists have been inclined to do in Europe.
Surely the main dependence of Socialists has to be on
the growth of working-class friendship across national
lines; on the development of a more effective program
for peace by Socialist parties; and on the coöperation of
nations which come under Socialist governments.

Meanwhile we in America who are profoundly concerned to prevent particular wars while we seek to change the system which is the mother of war cannot put our sole reliance in any political program. Our first and most important task is to concern ourselves with all those educational processes which tend to undermine the religion of profit and of nationalism. Nationalism itself was to no small extent a conscious creation. It had its prophets, it propagandists, its teachers. Man's new and saving loyalty to a federation of coöperative commonwealths likewise will require its prophets, its propagandists and teachers. It must have its poetry, its music, its cherished symbols.

But while this vitally necessary process of education is going on we shall be saved from war only by certain dogged and unshakable determinations. The first of these is that we who love peace must insist that the United States shall coöperate in everything that makes for peace and in nothing that makes or may make for war. Under no circumstances should we ever again be lured into war to establish peace. There is today a real danger that if war should break out between France and Germany a large section of public opinion in America would demand that we go to the aid of France to end that evil thing, anti-Semitic Fascism, in Germany. There is no exaggerating the evil, but surely in the light of the history of the First World War we must distrust international war as the way of justice or peace. A nation supposedly dedicated to democracy won the First World

War with the result that there is more and worse dictatorship than the Kaiser's abroad throughout the world. France backed by America might defeat Germany only to establish a French imperialism with new evils in it to curse mankind. Do not forget that French imperialism is actually and potentially a curse to mankind and that the anti-German phobia of the French did much to create the Nazi movement which for the first time since the war seems to justify the fear which had helped to make it.

Neither must the United States be led into any blind support of some scheme of action against a so-called aggressor nation. We should let it be understood that it is not our intention in advance to frustrate any economic actions by the League of Nations as against an aggressor nation by insisting upon our rights to trade with it. But the means of defining an "aggressor nation" in the light of present developments are by no means so sharp and accurate as to permit us to put our trust in a formula; we should support no consultative pact that goes beyond the promise to confer. Far better would be a resolution adopted in time of peace that the United States would not supply either belligerent in a great war with loans or munitions. This self-denying resolution would probably fail were we to wait to write it into law until war profits were dangled before the eyes of bankers and manufacturers and farmers as in the First World War. It might be adopted in advance and it should be accompanied by an aroused conscience among all workers against blood money derived from the production and sale of arms.

While this manuscript was at the printer's, talk of Russo-Japanese war became more explicit. Most Americans would, at least subconsciously, welcome such war as a "good war," a heaven-sent cure for depression better than the New Deal, and sell readily to both belligerents provided they have cash or good credit. Japan might be generally more unpopular than Russia, but average American opinion would bear up if both belligerents exhausted each other. There is no time to be lost in building up a public opinion against the sale of arms.

We cannot expect the whole American nation easily to take a rigorous stand for coöperation for peace and an absolute non-coöperation for war. No such result will be possible unless an increasing number of individuals and above all the working class as a whole will take a rigorous position of resistance to war. The most effective single means for stopping a particular war would be a general strike of workers against mobilization. The old debate concerning the utility of a general strike within a country as a political or revolutionary weapon is still undecided. It is, however, clear that in the moment of mobilization a general strike or a considerable approach to a general strike would be far more effective, and speedily effective, than a similar strike at a time when all the activities of a country were not focused on one task. The greatest single failure of Socialism as an international force prior to the First World War was its failure to perfect the machinery for such a strike. It might have gone far in Europe in 1914 where Socialist parties were strong. In spite of difficulties which have developed since the War there is still no better weapon than a general strike, and it is by no means impossible to familiarize workers with the idea if we set about it. The declaration of the British Labor Party in favor of such a strike ought to give an immense impetus to preparation for the use of this weapon of peace by other workers. It must be remembered that threat of such a strike was a potent factor in leading to the peaceful separation of Norway and Sweden at a time when the ruling classes in both countries were breathing forth war and destruction. Labor strikes or threat of strikes falling far short of a general strike were effective in restraining at critical junctures some of Lloyd George's post-War madness in Russia and at Constantinople. Strikes can and should be used, as soon as labor comes to consciousness of its own power and purpose, in order to stop the armament traffic.

It is wholly unlikely that in America or any other country the American labor movement or any other labor movement will take this determined stand of resistance to war unless there is an ever-increasing number of individuals who affirm that in the name of loyalty to everything they hold dear they will not be dragooned or conscripted into any war into which the greed or folly of profit makers and their political dupes may throw the nation. The great importance of war resistance is in preventing war. It will be almost impotent once war is declared. Then the conscientious objector will go to his doom. If enough of them face that doom like brave men their act will finally help to challenge and perhaps arrest the madness of a world. But the important thing is the preventive effect of war resistance. The rulers of the world will think twice before they will let their countries rush or tumble into a war which the young men will not fight.

There is a Communist argument that the avowed intention to turn new war into revolution will be more effective than resistance to war. Certainly the fact of possible revolution is a restraint against the declaration of war. Nevertheless there is more to be said for the utility of war resistance by the young than for a blanket declaration of intention at the right moment to turn foreign war into domestic revolution. Revolutionary situations are not made by individual agitators or mutineers; they arrive usually out of defeat in war. Before that can take place thousands of our armed revolutionaries who expect to practice the art of boring from within will have found themselves sent into battle either to kill their fellow men or to die before attack. For them to proclaim in advance their intentions to mutiny

will be to frustrate their work. For them to practice a
terrorism of blowing up troop trains or troop ships
would be to turn an hysterical popular wrath against all
pacifists and revolutionists and invite massacre. Our
young revolutionists themselves may be surprised to
find that once in the army they become subject to the
military insanity which so easily creeps over men. In the
First World War I knew, or knew of, scores if not hundreds of young men whose revolutionary or pacifist
ardor cooled extraordinarily fast when exposed to the
mass insanity of war. I presume the same thing would
happen to some war resisters. Yet the very number of
them and the firmness with which in advance they made
up their minds would give them a strength that their
older brothers lacked in the First World War. They
could erect for themselves psychological defenses
against propaganda greater than their comrades who
might go to the front hoping against hope that before
they themselves had died or spread devastation among
other workers the revolutionary moment might be at
hand. Beverley Nichols appeals to the young to fight for
no ruler and no country. Such a decision is not merely a
legitimate protest of the individual, asked to sacrifice
everything that life offers of honor, truth, beauty and
friendship to a homicidal mania. It is a valid method
of making particular wars more unlikely.

But not for an instant can we afford to forget that
behind all this it is our business to change the system

out of which these wars spring. The conquest of war
means the conquest of capitalism and nationalism. It is
not necessary to believe that with the passing of capitalism all danger of war will disappear. War as a social
institution had its beginning in history. There were
wars before capitalism, but there were no wars before
the organization of some form of predatory society.
The degree to which we can end a predatory society and
secure abundance through coöperation is the degree to
which war is made unlikely. It will not automatically
be abolished in a world in which some states, socialized
or semi-socialized, have immense advantage over less
fortunate or less intelligent nations. It will not be
ended automatically in a world where the masses are
kept in line by a fanatic mysticism in the service of one
party. The history of religion including the history of
the Communist religion makes that all too clear! But
without the end of the predatory society and divisive
nationalism there is no reasonable basis for peace. If
we can establish a federation of coöperative commonwealths without a resort to wholesale violence with its
legacy of passion and hate and without a complete surrender to the kind of dictatorship which creates the
possibility of a new tyranny of bureaucracy, then there
is every reason to expect an end of war. War can be
abolished before the abolition of police forces. It is
unscientific to assume that the end of war of itself
means the end of all force and violence, or that in order

to end war it is necessary completely to banish force and violence from earth.

The war situation is not a simple one-way proposition: get rid of capitalism or capitalist nationalism and thereby get rid of war. It is also true that the degree to which we can diminish the threat of war is the degree to which we can fight capitalist-nationalism without running foul of the kind of patriotism which is indivisibly connected with war rather than with peace. Without war patriotism it would be impossible to fool or coerce the masses into that acceptance of the national state as the bulwark of capitalism which now prevails not alone in Fascist states but in all of the non-Socialist world. If the events of the next few years bring the United States, England, and France to some form of Fascism rather than some form of Socialism there is no hope whatever for any long continuance of the unstable and troubled equilibrium men call peace.

This brings us logically to a consideration of the second way before us. That way is Fascism, and if our analysis of Fascism is half correct it will lead only to disaster and can only postpone catastrophe, a catastrophe which ultimately it may render more bitter. What is the outlook for Fascism in America? For a Fascism that is wholly imitative and habitually calls itself by that name there is a possibility but no great probability. For an organization of society essentially Fascist there is great probability except as it is consciously and deliberately fought off. That is to say there is a probability in America of a temporary stabilization of capitalism under a dictatorial or semi-dictatorial control of a state which in the guise of patriotism will make an emotional appeal to divert or to stupefy the masses whom it exploits. It is likely that besides the general appeal to nationalism Fascism to a greater or less degree will exploit other nationalistic and racial prejudices in America, possibly anti-Semitism, and certainly the dogma of white supremacy. The success of this Fascism will probably depend on its appearance not as a mere evolution of the control of the present dominant class but as a sort of middle-class revolution directed by some leader who assumes heroic proportions in the minds of the masses to whom he appeals. In other words, Fascism in America must do what it has done in Italy and Germany. Its appeal will be to that great mass of people who know that they are not really capitalists but who yet refuse to think of themselves as members of the working class.

An immense hope of preventing Fascism is, as I have already argued, the break-up of the strange psychology which holds together groups of those whose real interest is in the proper reward of labor, not of any kind of ownership. That section of the now dominant capitalist class which will work with the demagogue and subsidize him will continue in real power not merely as the result of intrigue and chicanery, but because the whole logic of a modern machine age is against the return to small-scale capitalism, plus some populist reforms.

How can this sort of development take place in the United States? The only wonder is that it has not proceeded more rapidly. Two major factors explain our immunity thus far to definite Fascist propaganda and organization. The first and less important is that while Americans were not satisfied with the result of the First World War they did not come out of it with such a sense of frustration as did the Italians, not with such a definite national inferiority complex as did defeated and exploited Germany. There has therefore developed no such touchy and self-conscious nationalism as Mussolini, and on an even greater scale Hitler, found ready to hand. Nevertheless, what I have already said about the world situation applies to America. As the Fascist ideal becomes more common in the world and Fascist states increase in number, the necessity of a national inferiority complex as a basis for Fascism becomes less and less. In place of it there is an emotional and contagious epidemic of rampant nationalism let loose in the world. The vainglory of what we call patriotism creates a psychological basis for Fascism.

The second and more important of the major factors, the lack of which has hindered the growth of American Fascism, is a popular distrust of a conventional capitalism on the one hand and fear of a working-class society on the other. We have already seen that in a sense the growth of Fascism has depended on the growth of Socialism and Communism. A misguided middle class has pushed its revolution as an alternative to a genuine revolution. Heretofore there has been so little conscious working-class organization of activity in America that neither our real ruling class nor their middle-class allies and dupes have felt the need of Fascism.

The present situation will not last. It is, as I have tried to make plain, an incorrect and dangerous use of words for the radical critic of the New Deal to call it Fascism. That is to commit the error of the boy who called "Wolf, wolf!" when there was no wolf. But the wolf will come. It has been the fundamental premise of our argument that capitalism cannot plan, or more accurately that capitalism with its deification of profit cannot long arrest the processes of its own disintegration. The degree to which it tries to plan for the social good is the degree to which it denies its own sanctions. If by the injection of an alien element of planning it obtains a temporary and partial degree of recovery it must sooner or later face the rising wrath of those whose productive labor creates the wealth the larger part of which is diverted under state capitalism to absentee owners. If, as seems more likely, the degree of the success of state capitalism scarcely wins a temporary respite, then it will become more necessary than ever to divert attention of both workers and the middle class itself from the colossal failure of the economic system. In either case the most convenient method of doing this will be an American adaptation of methods already used in Italy and Germany. The populace will be told that the real culprit is not capitalism but Wall Street or still better—if the demagogue can get away with it—an international banking conspiracy that is predominantly Jewish! Of course in the event of Fascist victory finance capital will be little if any more disturbed than in Germany. Its more far-seeing protagonists will subsidize the demagogue who aspires to a dictatorial rôle and the logic of capitalist concentration will continue.

Meanwhile the demagogue in his rôle as leader and hero will find plenty of passion and prejudice to exploit. Few countries are more vehemently nationalist than ours, and few countries, if any, have a more arrogant prejudice against all other races than that which we miscall white.

The eastern shore of Maryland, usually a peaceful enough social backwater, has within the last few months furnished an extraordinary record of lynchings, mob-violence and actual defiance of the governor of the state. A competent observer, Mr. Gerald Johnson, discussing the situation in the pages of the *New Republic* finds in the story an example of deep-seated impatience of an economically distressed district against Maryland's government by gentlemen. If he is right we have one more bit of evidence to add to the record of the Bleases, Bilbos, and Longs, to show that the character-istic Southern resentment takes far more certain toll of the Negro whom the Southern poor white has long regarded as inferior than of an upper class or a system which has exploited both the poor white and the Negro. This is a situation made to order for the Fascist dema-gogue.

But anti-Negro prejudice is not the only form of racial ill will in America, nor is it or any other racial or religious phobia spread with uniform intensity through-out the country. The Ku Klux Klan came to grief partly because of the difficulty of working together its three phobias against the Negro, the Jew, and the Pope. The very multitude of our American prejudices may help to save us! It will be very hard to find one satisfac-torily vivid and powerful devil to do for the American Fascist what the mythical Jew who is at one and the same time the world's great banker and the world's great Communist has done for the Nazis. Certainly the Negro cannot be blamed even in Mississippi for the sins either of J. P. Morgan or of Stalin, both of whom the anti-Semite by the logic of the madhouse identifies with the international Jewish ring!

It is not certain that Fascism in America will be predominantly anti-Semitic. The direct propaganda of the Nazis among Americans of German stock is of course anti-Semitic. So, too, is that weird combination of spiritualistic religion and unphilosophical radicalism which is typified by that thriving organization, the Silver Shirts. The White Shirts, or Crusaders for Economic Liberty, who see in the gold standard the source of all economic evil are more discreet. But it is likely that they are or will be anti-Semitic in the degree that will further their cause. Already their leader, George W. Christians, who is drilling his followers for a march on Washington quite in the Mussolini or Hitler tradition, has been acknowledged according to an article in the *New Republic* as a kind of kin spirit by a Nazi representative who closes a letter to him thus: "Let me salute you as you will be saluted in the days to come: 'Hail! Christians.' "

The Khaki Shirts, organized by that soldier of fortune, Art Smith, whose turbulent record stamps him as a paranoiac with delusions of grandeur, started out definitely to include Jews. Later according to a considerable body of testimony, Smith turned anti-Semite. Khaki Shirt meetings in Philadelphia and in New York resulted in riot and murder. In the latter city Smith accused an anti-Fascist named Athos Terzani of the murder although the victim was also an anti-Fascist. Terzani was triumphantly acquitted in a trial which showed that either the prosecutor's office in Queens County had some share in a deliberate frame-up or it was more cynically callous and incompetent than is usual even in America. One of the witnesses for the defense was a certain Samuel Wein, formerly a general under Art Smith. After partially corroborating Smith's testimony against Terzani before the Grand Jury, he testified in Terzani's behalf at the trial and definitely accused a Khaki Shirt of the murder. Mr. Wein said that he had originally borne false witness against Terzani in fear of Smith who had threatened that otherwise "he would kill all the Jews in America." The Judge interposed, "Did you believe that?" to which Wein replied, "Well, I didn't want to be the first." Whatever else this incident proves, it clearly shows a break in the organization on the Semitic issue. Still another quasi-Fascist organization, the so-called Order of '76, gives to its supposedly patriotic activities an anti-Semitic slant.

It is not likely, then, that any of these or their mush-room rivals is destined to be *the* American vehicle of Fascism. It is not that they are intellectually preposterous—so was Hitler's budding movement in the eyes of intelligent Germans—it is rather that these organizations have not discovered a genuinely national appeal or anyone resembling a national hero. They are symptoms of a deep and ominous disease rather than causes of it. If and when an American Fascism comes, it may owe more to various organizations of veterans or of the Reserve Officers Associations than to any of the numerous groups designated by the kind of shirts they wear.

Unquestionably an American Fascism will have its

own military or semi-military organization. It is one of the evil legacies of the war that popular organizations in America turn to this military form to a degree undreamed of before the war. Mussolini's Black Shirts gave a further impetus to this military form of uniformed organizations in a country where men had previously been content to escape drab reality by becoming Eagles, or Moose, or Red Men, or Tall Cedars of Lebanon.

So far as anti-Semitism goes, it is possible to hope that the shocking excesses of the Nazis will serve in America as a warning against Fascism rather than as an incitement to it. There is, as there has been, anti-Jewish feeling in America, but in an organized form it is scarcely on the increase in a country which has recently elected Jewish governors in its first and third most populous states. What is disquieting is that now and then even in labor circles, for instance in the organ of the Progressive Miners of America, one discovers echoes of anti-Semitism and a tendency to blame the sins of an exploiting class upon a particular race. In certain strikes of sweat-shop workers in districts where the employers were Jewish and the workers Gentile, the cry has been heard, "Give us a Hitler."˙ In this case the leadership of the union organizing the workers was predominantly Jewish so that the anti-Semitic issue was easily met. That may not always be true.

On the whole the racial discrimination which taints

American labor unionism is anti-Negro. It was also vehemently anti-Asiatic prior to Asiatic exclusion. By now white workers of various races have learned to accept one another. Labor unionism, however, has not produced a labor solidarity which is as emotionally strong as certain types of racial, national, and religious solidarity have been. The great outpouring of New York's workers in protest against Hitlerism was under the banner of the Jewish race, not of the labor movement. "Workers of the World, Unite," is a slogan yet to be fulfilled even in that section of one continent which we too boastfully call America.

Paradoxically it is true, as we have already seen, that the comparative weakness of labor organization in America has delayed the coming of Fascism because it has retarded the growth of fear in the owning class. But that class is easily alarmed and is likely to turn to some form of Fascism long before labor is well enough organized to fight it on even terms unless there is a tremendous and successful organization of working-class sentiment which will include large sections of those now middle class in their point of view. This sort of organization is likely to be made more difficult because there is a type of labor leader, sometimes not to be distinguished from a racketeer, who finds it easier to build his own syndicate—to use the term in Mussolini's sense—in collusion with certain employers than to build a true union. I have referred to this tendency in earlier pages of this book. Since they were written the organization of retail clerks in New York has furnished some striking examples of what can happen. One of the union officials, a man named Denise, hired an engineer named Stiner to organize, especially in chain grocery stores, company unions with A. F. of L. sanction. When the *World Telegram* exposed what was going on Stiner was promptly repudiated as having exceeded his authority; but, as this paragraph is written, the union is still refusing a proper investigation of the degree of complicity of some of its own officers with Stiner personally, and their use of practices essentially not much different from Stiner's. This sort of labor unionism paves the way for Fascism rather than fights it no matter how many anti-Fascist resolutions the A. F. of L. may adopt.

One more circumstance facilitates the development of an American Fascism. It is the growing contempt for that imperfect political system which Americans have been taught to call democracy. For some years there has been a carefully cultivated contempt for Congress. Now the worst that can be said for Congress is that it fairly represents the confused American mind and that it can be manipulated by high-pressure politics of certain interested groups. The best that can be said for Congress is that in matters of social legislation, including taxation, in the years 1919-33 it has been more enlightened and done more to help and less to hurt the country than the executive or the Supreme Court. Yet it has been made the whipping boy for the sins of government. If one finds a Congress Street or a Congress Hotel in America one can be sure that it is respectable with age. We moderns do not name even a dog after Congress. This feeling against Congress, justified in part, but only in part, may easily play into the hands of a dictator who will manipulate the Constitution or defy it for Fascist ends.

I have been assuming that eventually there will be one national Fascist movement with one leader. This is not altogether certain. Fascism in Italy and Germany has enhanced nationalism as against regionalism. The United States is a bigger country and it is barely possible that we shall get sectional movements of varying degrees of Fascism or anti-Fascism. The farmers of the Middle West have more than once talked a kind of economic secession from the United States. The North Dakota Legislature during Hoover's time had a resolution favoring virtual secession put before it. Governor Langer of North Dakota under the Roosevelt Administration put an embargo on wheat from the state until it reached a certain price. Governor Murray of Oklahoma earlier took a similar step to stop the production of oil. Does not this suggest that China may not be the only great nation capable of regional disintegration? At least there are enough possibilities for this sort of thing to make it foolhardy to believe that necessarily or even probably a particular Fascist coup in Washington or Chicago or New York would carry the nation with it.

The object of this argument is not to prove the inevitability of Fascism, much less of any particular type of Fascism. We have time to fight it. There are obstacles in the way of its success. The American press which partly for selfish reasons of its own has manifested a lively interest in "liberty" as opposed to a code has lately been less enthusiastic than was its wont about Mussolini. Such conservative papers as the *Chicago Tribune* and the *New York Herald-Tribune* have commented with appropriate horror on some sample Fascist instructions to the press of Italy made public by that little Italian-American anti-Fascist paper *La Stampa Libra*. The fiction of Italian prosperity under Fascism is wearing thin and the fiction of German prosperity never got well started. Further economic depression in Italy or Germany even if it were not attended by open rebellion would take the lustre off any European Fascism. Capitalism's last stand would have to adopt its own "made in America" nostrums. Lawrence Dennis' attempt to intellectualize American Fascism in *The Awakener* would have to put over a formula as American as was William Jennings Bryan.

Nevertheless there is very small probability that the ultimate disintegration of Fascism will advance fast enough or obviously enough to save the country from Fascism unless there is an active struggle against it.

With an insistence greater than that wherewith Cato preached the destruction of Carthage, we must urge that *the alternative to the totalitarian state is the coöperative commonwealth, the alternative to some sort of Fascism is some sort of Socialism.* If Socialism is to be an alternative to Fascism rather than its possible successor it will not be of the Communist type. Despite all the sincerity of Communist opposition to Fascism the continued emphasis of its leaders upon dictatorship and violence plays into Fascist hands. A Communist dictatorship may promise far more for the future of mankind than the Fascist dictatorship. But in any near period of time if the mass of Americans come to feel that the choice is between American dictatorship and Russian, or between the patriotic violence of Fascism and what they are bound to consider the greater violence of Communism, there can be no question that they will turn to Fascism far more readily than did the Germans. The whole problem of democracy and dictatorship and the rôle of violence in social change is, of course, not solved by what I have said. It is, however, worth emphasizing that radicals who believe in the necessity of dictatorship and large-scale violence are in America postponing their hope of salvation to an indefinite future. Americans have all too violent a tradition. In the land of gangsterism, the third degree, and lynchings, he who beats down whatever protections we have built up for civil liberties and democratic ideals and methods is paving the way for Fascist violence and dictatorship far more congenial in its objects and methods to American traditions and folkways than orthodox Communism can ever be. It is hard to see how any honest and acute observer can accept the inevitability of the Communist method of obtaining power in America without postponing it to those of our children who may survive Fascism or world war or a mixture of both. The immediate alternative to Fascism is the rapid growth of a democratic Socialism which will not be too weak or too cowardly to carry on the struggle which lies before it, which will not forever subordinate Socialism to a mechanical and rigid conception of democracy, but will present itself as the fulfillment of what is best in the democratic tradition and the guarantor of a heaven which can be reached without compelling men to pass through the lowest circles of a hell of violence and disorder. It is to some of the problems of that sort of Socialism that we must turn as to our only way of escape.

CHAPTER IX

TOWARD THE COÖPERATIVE
COMMONWEALTH

IN terms of common sense there is no case at all against the Socialist notion that the great natural resources ought to be our common possession, managed for the common use, and that the tools which require integrated operation by specialized groups, and cannot reasonably be owned as the carpenter owns his tools, should not be owned by absentees who make a profit out of ownership. They, too, should be a common possession managed for use, not profit. Already we have the resources and the equipment which if operated with reasonable efficiency would give the average American family an income variously estimated at from five to twenty thousand dollars yearly. And this on a weekly schedule of hours of necessary work averaging well under the thirty-hour week which is now labor's goal. None of this work need involve the grim back-breaking toil or the hourly dangers to life and limb which the stokers in an old-fashioned steamship or the workers in the older type of steel mill accepted as men accept the weather.

Such a society would let no man own land by virtue of a title deed but it might easily give more secure and peaceful tenure on a particular piece of land than the average farmer or small home owner now enjoys. Conceivably the collective society might involve a stultifying degree of regimentation, but not necessarily. Security against poverty, war, and unemployment, and emancipation from fear of the men or corporations who today own the vitally necessary jobs, together with the great increase in leisure, ought to give men a great release of energy and encourage rather than discourage the highest types of self-expression. Industrially the basic initiative of this society would be the initiative of the engineer and the administrator rather than the promoter. But so it is today—under circumstances, however, where honor and reward go to the speculator and the promoter. For valuable work well done not only would there be the incentive of honor and power, but perhaps certain extra material remuneration which would by no means involve the return of the profit system. Our developing science of psychology and education would guide our young people far better than they can be guided in our haphazard and predatory world to that work for which they are best fitted. That guidance would fall far short of conscription. So great are our powers of production and so rapidly can they be increased that we could afford a considerable variety of consumers' choice even at the cost of some theoretical waste. We should not have to wait through gaunt years while we provided ourselves with machinery at the price of hunger as the Russians have done. And yet when Margaret and Corliss Lamont and others remind us of this fact and argue that therefore the revolution in America may be less long and costly than in Russia most of us listen incredulously. Why?

The answer is, of course, to be found in terms of our existing social system and the pressure of its ideals and institutions upon us. If we could start in possession of our present mechanical equipment and resources and otherwise with a clean slate no one would think of building so cruel and crazy a world as the one we live in. The trouble is, we can't start with that clean slate. We live in a country where the dominant ruling class, with few exceptions, is not going to abandon its power, its wealth and prestige, even temporarily for an adventure in coöperation. Its ownership gives it possession of most of the engines of power and propaganda. It can rally to its support a surprising number of those who own a little or who hope to own a little or whose callings in life seem to them bound up with the *status quo*. These range all the way from the household servants of the rich through various of the luxury trades up to advertising men and a certain section, at least, of the clergy and the teaching profession. The very circumstances which make an intelligent socialized collectivism necessary, make the average individual or the average group more reluctant to take the risk of changing the system which has to be changed as a whole, unless it is to be reduced to worse chaos. Hence it is that audiences which listen with ill-concealed impatience to almost any and every intellectual defense of capitalism can usually be trusted to vote Republican or Democrat, certainly not Socialist or Communist.

Radicals often miss the point with consequent ill effect upon their tactics and propaganda by talking as if their enemy were the sheer power of a relatively small owning class. That power in terms of physical or mental force is not great, save for the circumstances which seem to unite so many of the exploited to the cause of the exploiter. Of these circumstances the greatest is the time element. We are dealing with dissatisfied men, but men grown used to chains and twilight. Even courageous men have to live somehow. It is all very well to picture the joys of a brave new world, but how do we get there? Where and when do we eat on the way? We may cheer for the man who promises us heaven but we work for the man who promises us a dollar more a week. In some respects the Socialist is at a disadvantage with the preacher who promises "pie in the sky by and by." For the Socialist can offer to this generation no assurance of immortality in which its members can share the joys of the coöperative commonwealth wherein, after years of struggle, some men and women will delight. It is this problem of the transitional period, the necessity of living while we fight for a better life, the task—to use a familiar illustration—of keeping the trains running while we rebuild the tracks and the terminals, which determines most of the present-day differences in Socialist tactics. We might get farther if we would recognize this plain truth and stop clothing our differences in the dialectics of Marxist theology.

For instance, consider the perennial question of violence in the social revolution which has helped, as we have seen, to divide Socialists and Communists. Let us get away for a few minutes from party recriminations and general affirmations: violence is evil, violence is necessary, and so forth. What kind of violence do we envisage? Both Socialists and Communists are agreed on the dangerous folly of the premature violence of sporadic insurrection. For that the common man was never less well equipped than today. The old family rifle and the street barricade are no weapons to use against airplanes, poison gas and machine guns. There are four conceivable types of violence on a considerable scale which might be used in a revolutionary struggle:

1. Discontented soldiers might turn foreign war into sharp and swift revolution. This is scarcely likely to happen except after defeat in war and under circumstances which make it no hope at all for the present generation, but only an eventual way of possible escape for survivors out of previous agony almost beyond endurance. Nor is there any certainty that this military revo-

lution would be Socialist or Communist in purpose and led with the brilliance of Lenin and Trotsky.

2. Civil war, more horrible in its destructive power for a nation with oceans as its boundaries than any foreign war is likely to be. Such a civil war might follow foreign war or might arise out of the domestic struggle in America itself. Whatever its original purposes it would be fought with incredible cruelty in our nation with its tradition of sadistic violence. It would probably give rise to one or more military dictatorships which might make the much abused Congress the symbol of a lost golden age even to some of our radicals, intellectual and otherwise, to whom violence now seems so inevitable and perhaps romantically so desirable.

3. A sharp and relatively bloodless *coup d'etat* of the sort successfully engineered by Trotsky in the Bolshevik revolution. As we have previously observed in discussing the possibility of the break-up of the American Republic, there is no single city, certainly not Washington, New York or Chicago, the capture of which would give the victors control over the nation. The attempt at any *coup d'etat,* which might be something more than the final gesture in a long campaign of organization, education, and political action, would likely be the signal either for a regional partition of America or for a great counter-revolution against the party attempting the *coup d'etat.* Even a Fascist movement in America would probably follow the tactics of Hitler

rather than of Mussolini if it were to be successful. That is to say, the violence would be the violence of the bully who coerces men and women at the polls, rather than of the soldier.

4. The final possible use of violence is of a different sort. Its purpose would be to defend or preserve that which was already won or on the point of being won at the polls and by the effective use of the power of labor on the economic field. A Socialist government might conceivably use such violence sharply and decisively against a ruling class which refused a surrender of power or which sabotaged the new order. In all probability a party which acquired power or a considerable degree of power in the state by means recognized as democratic, would have an immense psychological and practical advantage in getting the support of part at least of the military forces and the police —far more than if it were recognized from the outset as violently revolutionary.

To be a Tolstoyan in one's opposition to violence one must go all the way with Tolstoy in his general view of life and in his refusal to accept the fruits of the organized exploitation of an upper-class state which ruthlessly uses violence for its own end. All that the rest of us can do is steadily to seek means for the necessary struggle to capture power which involve the minimum of coercion and especially of violent coercion. We can at least recognize the new problem that the extraordinary means of destruction now put in our hands has created for us. We can hang on jealously to such positive gains as the notion of democracy has given us in substituting even partially the vote for the gun or the sword. In doing this we need not be uncritical of our present mechanical and hypocritical democracy, but the contrary. No Socialist party, for instance, can permit its followers to identify democracy with rigid constitutionalism or to encourage the delusion that the present scheme of government in America is suitable to the new society or the transition to it. An effective mandate for Socialism must be a mandate for change in the forms of government and many of the processes under which today the rule of privilege masquerades as democracy. To this we may return.

The point which here is of vital importance is simply this: in our complex and immensely vulnerable society no violence promises us anything better than a deeper descent into a hell of our own making, unless, as Reinhold Niebuhr has suggested, it bears some resemblance to the violence of a surgical operation rather than of wholesale butchery, a violence limited in duration and extent, so that the healing processes can soon begin. The less the violence and the hate the more secure will be the coöperative commonwealth which shall arise. He who because of discouragement over the slowness of peaceful methods and the ruthlessness of an owning class tries to escape reality and encourages the workers who have not yet formed a political party of their own to see themselves as victors in some future apocalypse of violence knows not what he does. In the immediate task which lies before us the last way to get workers with hand and brain to achieve an effective solidarity is to minimize the ultimate usefulness of everything except the machine gun and the bomb. This position one can hold with deep sincerity and yet not ask workers, as do so many preachers, to adopt a Tolstoyan rôle which we—and they—have never expected of governments or of the ruling class.

There is a second important issue which is often discussed in curiously unrealistic terms. I refer to the important question: how shall we transfer natural resources and the great tools of production from private to public ownership, by compensation or confiscation? In the first place the question which I have put in its usual form does not present all the alternatives. In March, 1933, Mr. Roosevelt might have nationalized or even socialized the banking system without wholesale confiscation or any process of compensation as expensive as has been involved in the loans or gifts which the R. F. C. has extended to banks and railroads to keep them in private hands. Mr. Roosevelt had in his grasp all the elements of a public-owned banking system. The government had a large share of ownership of the Federal Reserve Banks and ultimate control of the system. Any equity of stockholders in most privately owned banks had been wiped out by the crisis, and those banks which were still solvent or might easily be made solvent could have remained in government possession to be linked to the new system. Finally, the government already had a Postal Savings system reaching into every hamlet. Out of these elements it could have built its own system with carefully segregated thrift and commercial accounts. It could have operated the system under a Federal Reserve Board to control the short-time credits of commercial banking and a Credit Board to guide for social ends, rather than for the monetary gain of profit makers, the use of credit which is itself a social creation. It could have permitted sound credit unions which have had an enviable record in the depression to enter the system. It could have encouraged municipalities and perhaps states to establish banks as members of the system. It might even have permitted strong banks, whose owners had a sound equity in them, to continue to operate as members of the system, but under such stringent control as would guarantee their rapid absorption into social ownership. A plan like this would have laid the basis for an efficient handling of the money problem and would have been a principal factor in a general scheme of production for use. And all of this might have been done without either confiscation or compensation on the scale which the words usually suggest to excited debaters.

It had been recognized, at least since Henry George

wrote *Progress and Poverty,* that the government as the agent of society could wipe out private landlordism and establish in reality the social ownership of land by the simple principle of a tax expropriating the rental value of the land apart from improvements. In the process, tenure of land might be made more rather than less secure for those who live on it. I do not believe, as did Mr. George, that this land tax is a sole and sufficient answer to our agricultural problem. In regard to agriculture we shall have to build sound coöperatives and establish socialized marketing of what the farmer buys and what he sells. We shall have to work out a plan, in the light of foreign as well as domestic trade, for the proper use of land. Again the point that I am making is that we can work out a program for agriculture without reducing farmers to the status of factory workers through compulsory collectivization by confiscation. An intelligent handling of the problem of farm debt and taxation will give us our leverage. There will be, in the large sense of the word, compensation for the farmers, but it will not be at the price which an indefinite continuance of the process of subsidizing an artificial scarcity will entail.

Another possibility which involves neither compensation nor confiscation is the independent development of mineral lands and water power already in the possession of government, somewhat along the lines of the Tennessee Valley Development, which would be more surely successful if it were part of a general plan of socialization. Finally, it must be remembered that the advocate of compensation as opposed to confiscation always means *compensation plus taxation.* And what that implies we shall presently see.

But when all this has been said, it is still true that there is and must be a choice between compensation and confiscation in the case of railroads, steel mills, coal mines and a host of other things. Concerning these, no intelligent Socialist can repudiate confiscation in principle. Their value is the creation of labor, and that labor, whether of hand or brain, has been to an amazingly small extent the labor of their present owners. The worth of these great possessions is a social heritage to which the labor of the living steadily adds. Confiscation for social purposes rightfully carried out, is restitution. There is no question that it is the method which workers must and will use if the resistance of an owning class compels them to use force. There is no question that it will be the short and easy way to cut the Gordian knot of property rights if and when a smoothly functioning Socialist government can promptly take over all such property and extend to those who have heretofore found in ownership of it protection for their children and their own old age a finer and surer protection which a well-run coöperative commonwealth will provide for the young, the invalid, and the old.

The case, then, for compensation as against confiscation does not rise from immutable principle, but from a balancing of present advantages. Most Socialists believe in compensation plus taxation rather than confiscation, because they believe that today we are not ready to take over at one act all the great means of production and run them smoothly, and that piecemeal confiscation of the sort which the government would likely apply invites confusion and counter-revolution. Let us see how things would work out. A Socialist government in any near future would begin by nationalizing at first a comparatively few basic industries and services which have already been largely monopolized or which should promptly be monopolized. Other things would wait— some of them of a non-essential sort for a considerable time. By this piecemeal confiscation the owners of certain types of stocks or bonds would lose everything, while owners of other types of property would still continue to enjoy to some degree the fruits of ownership. The principle of this piecemeal confiscation would not be the wealth or the wickedness of those whose property was taken; indeed, the things that a Socialist government would likely take over first are precisely things, like our public utilities, in which the savings of little men have been invested directly or through insurance companies and savings banks, for the protection of their old age or the help of their dependents. What do you think would happen if the holders of insurance policies or the direct investors, let us say in railroads, should lose everything by confiscation, while the owners of printing plants, clothing manufacturers, or beauty parlors, for a longer or a shorter time, continued their ownership, subject only to such taxation and regulation as might be imposed upon them? Of course, such discrimination or the threat of it would rally everyone who owned something or who hoped to own something under the war cry, "No confiscation." Clearly we are not likely to be able to take over and successfully operate all industry as quickly as we can and should take over the commanding heights of industry. Ramsay MacDonald, after his betrayal of Socialism, carried a working-class district in England by frightening the voters with a groundless fear that his old associates of the Labor Party would make their little savings bank deposits as worthless as German marks in the great deflation. Imagine what a similar propaganda could do in America. Or, if you prefer to speculate on the past rather than on the future, consider how much better all of us, North and South, white and black, would have been if the freedom of slaves, unjustly held in bondage, had been purchased with money rather than with blood and hate.

I heard Mr. Lincoln Steffens in a public address express a kind of half-formed hope that the Communists might build their new world by the aid of migratory workers like the cotton pickers then on strike, who were not contaminated by the possession of property. Unquestionably, propertyless cotton pickers have their place in building the coöperative commonwealth, but it is a fantastic sentimentality to suppose that in a country where the idea of property not only in consumption but in production goods is so widespread, and its benefits distributed, however imperfectly, through insurance policies and savings bank accounts, we shall make progress at any time, short of a complete collapse of the whole system or of the complete perfection of a Socialist scheme, by threatening the little man with the loss of what protection he now has or thinks he has. Socialism must appeal to masses well above the economic status of migratory workers as definitely bettering their condition in a short space of time, or else it will not appeal at all. This is not to deny the capacity of men to sacrifice for a cause or the value of an appeal to it. It is recognizing the limits of such sacrifice.

Fortunately there is a way of handling the problem of compensation, which surmounts some of its worse evils and is tactically superior to piecemeal confiscation. Coal mines, railroads and the like can be acquired by substituting, not government bonds, but the bonds of the new socially owned corporation for a reasonable valuation of outstanding securities. If that valuation were to be the market cost of the stocks of most coal companies during the depression the price would not be great! These bonds would bear a rate of interest less rather than more than four per cent, which is a good average return on so-called gilt-edge securities. They would be retired progressively in a period not to exceed thirty years, perhaps by annual payments in reduction of the principal. Payments on them could not be reinvested in the ownership of resources and industries which the state would be rapidly acquiring. They would carry absolutely no claim to any voice in the control of the socialized property, and they would be subject to taxation of precisely the sort which would be imposed upon all capital. Income from them would not be tax-exempt, but would have to be computed by the recipient in his income tax returns. They would be subject to the inheritance tax and to the capital levy. This capital levy would apply to all possessors of wealth and would be levied according to their ability to pay, not according to the source from which their wealth was derived. The owner of a chain of beauty parlors would pay equally with the owner of stock in railroads which had been converted into bonds of a government-owned corporation. A capital levy would be carefully graduated; it could be paid, if necessary, on the installment plan, in money, in government bonds, which would then be retired, or in stocks of the corporations, which sooner or later the government might desire to socialize. If a capital levy rather than a general scaling down of capital structure were used to reduce the preposterous burden of debt now resting upon many private corporations and some individuals, it would mean that for this reduction of debt the government would receive a share in ownership or control or both. Such a reduction of the farmer's indebtedness by the government out of the proceeds of a capital levy or an inheritance tax should be used to facilitate transfer of title to the government, with occupancy guaranteed to the present possessor, so long as he desires to cultivate the soil with preferential right of his heirs to succeed him.

Recently a variant of the idea of confiscation has been discussed. It is proposed by constitutional amendment or otherwise to end *absentee* ownership. The idea at first is attractive but it would hit the little man through savings banks and it might let some great exploiters like Henry Ford go relatively free on the ground that whatever they are or are not they are not absentee owners. They do run their own business. Absentee ownership is about the least defensible feature of capitalism and its growth marks the disintegration of the system. Nevertheless the trouble lies with the *private*, not necessarily with the *absentee*, ownership of that which should be publicly owned and managed for use, not profit.

The candid man must admit that some scheme of compensation plus taxation does help to perpetuate for almost another generation the concept and institution of ownership, not merely of the things one uses—which is legitimate—but of the things that others must use in order to produce wealth for society. A perfect social plan put into effect after one act of confiscation would end this concept and its anti-social influence on man. The perfect plan is not now available and the effort to apply piecemeal confiscation against bitter and violent opposition is far more likely to perpetuate false ideals and a lust for property than an orderly plan for rapid socialization, beginning with key industries, in which compensation plus taxation plays a major but not an exclusive part.

Many of these arguments about the rôle of violence and confiscation in the social revolution would find their answer and their proper proportion if we could do the one thing of primary importance; that is, to arouse in the hearts of the masses a passionate desire for the coöperative commonwealth and a belief in the possibility of its attainment within our own time. The deeper and the more widespread this revolution in men's thoughts and desires the surer and the less violent will be the outward revolution in our social structure. Men who will not be fooled or bribed or easily coerced into the service of an owning class will be surprised how little physical force that class has at its disposal to impose its will and how far it is itself from any such inner unity or intelligence as will make it invincible.

This coöperative commonwealth of its nature implies a sharing of work and the ownership of the necessary tools for work. Its whole culture will be the culture of a community of workers, not of a community of exploiters and the exploited. Its appeal is peculiarly an appeal to the unprivileged and the dispossessed. It cannot be achieved without arousing a working-class consciousness and a loyalty to a fraternity of workers big enough to include all those who do the useful work of the world and minister to the fullness of human life.

If this need of a new sort of loyalty to integrate our common life is the primary necessity, it is almost of equal importance to have an immediate program for taking care of the urgent wants of men and women and children without compelling them to sell their glorious birthright for a mess of potage. Socialism in Germany and England suffered less because of difficulties of procedure inherent in democracy than for lack of a vigorous and well-thought-out program, aggressively pushed under able leadership.

All that I have said implies an importance in America of an immediate program of social insurance, unemployment relief, agricultural aid, and the guarantee of civil liberty, including the right of all workers to organize. It certainly implies that immediate concern for peace and an immediate program for preserving it, such as we have already discussed. But the essential feature of any immediate program for Socialism which is of value, and the one thing which will make an immediate program a sound beginning of the transitional period, is a redistribution of the national income on a basis that will give to workers collectively the fruits of their labor.

Without this there is no cure for unemployment, bitter poverty, recurring crises and ultimate collapse. Now a kind of patchwork job of limited redistribution of income can be done, as everybody knows, by a program of high taxation on the rich and various social benefits for the poor. But this can never reach to the heart of our problem. Redistribution of the national income should not be a process of intervention by government to restore to the robbed a small portion of what has been taken from them. It should be a process of ending exploitation and establishing a scheme of things in which production is naturally and logically for use rather than for the private profit of an owning class. There is no such scheme of things which does not require social ownership. It follows that the immediate and essential objective of any desirable program must be the socialization and proper management of key industries. Socialization is not identical with nationalization. Increasingly it must be on an international scale. Immediately it may include ownership and operation by bona fide consumers' coöperatives. But practically the next steps toward socialization will require a process by which the national government will take over ownership. Such nationalization will fall short of socialization if, for instance, railroads should be taken over for military purposes, or banks in order to make a state capitalism more efficient. True socialization can never lose sight of the great purpose of shared abundance.

Just what industries should be nationalized first, just how they shall be acquired, and how conducted, are questions to which the same answer cannot be given yesterday, today, and forever. The principles of Socialism are sure and unchanging; their application is a matter of strategy to be worked out in the light of the existing situation, the strength of our own forces and the forces of the enemy. On March 4, 1933, a Socialist administration ought to have begun with the socialization of banking. In rapid succession it would have taken over railroads, coal mines, and the power and oil industries. Then, as I have already indicated, it would have turned its attention to other monopolies. Any worthwhile agricultural program will compel the government to set up socialized marketing agencies and to take over and run as a public non-profit-making organization the dairy trust and probably the packing houses. In some cases it might not be necessary or desirable for the government to acquire all the existing property of, let us say, the power corporations or the dairy trust. It might condemn those facilities necessary for building up a great and economical system in conjunction with resources and facilities already in possession of governmental agencies, federal, state, and local. The methods by which the transfer of ownership can be brought about I have already discussed in discussing the question of confiscation.

In all socialized industry, administration should be

functional, not superimposed by the political state. The railroads ought not to be run under a cabinet officer like the Postmaster General, but under a board of directors representing both the workers who invest their brains, their brawn, their very lives in the service, and the traveling public. Since there is and always will be some difference of interest between the workers in a particular industry and other workers who consume the product or use the services of that industry, both groups should be represented on the highest administrative authority.

All socialized industries and other industries not yet socialized but operating under codes, should be subject to the general strategy of an expert planning board. Compensation or remuneration for work done in socialized industries would not, in the transitional period, be absolutely uniform. There would not be the fantastic salaries and bonuses paid to high executives, but there would be special remuneration for especially valuable service or for work into which it is better to attract desirable workers than to conscript them. In a world of abundance the whole problem of the precise remuneration will become less and less important. There will be enough and to spare for all. Equality of income may be the ultimately desirable goal. More and more we shall depend upon incentives of honor, the desire for power, the creative urge, and the principle of mutual aid to stimulate men's efforts.

These incentives operate today. Their success has been recorded in the rapid industrialization of Russia. Even in capitalist America they, rather than unbridled cupidity, have kept things going. Government-owned enterprises, yes, government itself, operated with some deference to public service has made in these years of depression a record better than business. Tammany cost New York less than Wall Street, and Jimmy Walker gave us a better show than Charlie Mitchell, while it lasted.

While it is wholly desirable that the state as an agent of a dominant class shall give way to a true commonwealth in which coercion shall steadily yield to coöperation, there is no question that the program we have outlined requires the capture of the political state. In America it is at least as likely that this essential capture of power and its use for social ends can be the achievement of a workers' democracy as of any sort of dictatorship. And the more we can keep of civil liberty and the tolerance that has been associated with democracy, the happier will be the transition period and the surer its victories. Nevertheless, our struggle must be for the capture of all power. The achievement of Socialism in our time cannot be accidental or haphazard; it will not be the gift of some "Gabriel over the White House" or of this or any future Roosevelt in the White House. We shall not wake up to discover to our pleased surprise that without knowing it or consciously working for it, we have reached the coöperative commonwealth under its own or any other name.

It does not follow, however, that particular concessions in the matter of taxation, social insurance, or the nationalization of particular industries, extorted by pressure from a government which the workers have not yet captured, is a mere reformist measure of no account in itself and perhaps even a hindrance, used like the apples of Atalanta to divert labor from running its course and winning its race. These measures, if they are useful in themselves, and if they are got by direct pressure of the workers, are not to be despised. Some of the machinery that we are getting under the New Deal will be useful for the easier achievement either of the coöperative commonwealth or of the totalitarian state, depending entirely on which group presses forward to power.

Any effective capture and use of political power will require a drastic overhauling of our governmental machinery. No coöperative commonwealth can be operated so long as power is divided between a federal government and forty-eight states along geographical lines, and as a result of historical accidents, which divisions of power have absolutely no relevance to industries already organized on a national scale. Still less can a transitional period be managed under our archaic threefold division of powers: executive, legislative, and a judicial oligarchy of nine old men who sit on the Su-

preme Court Bench. It is to Mr. Roosevelt's credit that
he has found a way to diminish in practice those states'
rights that were in reality workers' wrongs, and perhaps
to get around the court which has made the Fourteenth
Amendment to the Constitution not a charter of freedom to slaves but of privilege to an exploiting class. But
it is not yet certain that the Supreme Court will tolerate
the New Deal. It is certain that today it would declare
Socialism unconstitutional.[1] The best answer to this
threat is at once to work for a Constitutional Amendment giving Congress power to pass all needful social
and economic legislation, including the right to lay a
capital levy. Fortunately, recent history has proved that
amending the Constitution is not as difficult as it had
once seemed. This particular amendment is necessary
to make American democracy in this emergency something more than a mask for class rule intrenched in the
Constitution. It affords the best chance we have for
peaceful progress in Socialism.

It goes without saying that such an amendment is not
enough to save the situation. One of the earliest tasks
of a Socialist government must be to bring about a new
and simpler constitution. It is my personal opinion that

[1] The famous Minnesota case, decided, since this chapter was written,
by a five to four decision in favor of the power of the state to declare
a moratorium on mortgage payments, is encouraging as far as it goes.
It does not necessarily apply to the power of the Federal Government—
and what a business it is that we should be dependent for progressive
social control over property on the opinion of some one lawyer who
casts the deciding vote!

authority in the coöperative commonwealth should rest in a single-chambered congress, not too large for proper discussion, to which the executive should be responsible. Voters should vote for a certain number of Congressmen to be elected in the nation at large and a somewhat greater number to be elected one for each district. To these should be added another group not over a third of the whole, to be elected by workers to represent their own industries. By and large the permanent interests of workers as consumers and citizens can best be furthered by representatives chosen on the geographical principle; their permanent interest as producers, by representatives chosen on the occupational principle. It is not necessary to assume that these representatives of different interests will always vote in blocs. Responsible political parties should make nominations both for geographic and occupational representatives and pledge them to carry out a party platform; and yet, with party responsibility, we should obtain the advantage of having legislation worked out in the light of a double point of view. This double type of representation in one chamber, where party responsibility still prevails, is preferable to the division of authority between two chambers or two parliaments, one chosen by the occupational and the other by the geographic principle. Between them there would always be a struggle for supremacy.

The principal difficulty in this plan is to obtain under it the strong executive leadership which in a transitional period would be necessary. I admit the difficulty which, however, will tend to diminish as we pass out of the transitional period. Even during the transitional it may be lessened: (1) By properly developed party responsibility—remember that Stalin owes his immense authority to a party and not to a government position, which is a suggestive though not a perfect analogy to what might happen under a democratic government; and (2) by insisting that details of administration, apart from general principles and the formulation of an economic plan, should be the work of administrative bureaus, and directorates of socialized industries, and the supreme economic council, rather than Congress itself. The relation of the economic council to Congress will require much thought and possibly some experimentation. Obviously the economic council should be composed of experts and should be protected from sudden gusts of congressional displeasure. Nevertheless, if there is to be any sort of democracy at all, the choice of broad policies which will effect economic strategy must be made by Congress as representative of the workers in their rôle as producers and consumers, and Congress in the last analysis must have power to enforce both upon the general economic council and upon the national executive its final decision, unless and until that decision itself is altered by the electorate. The concern of the electorate in modern society cannot reasonably be with the homely details which occupied the attention of an old-fashioned town meeting. It can only be with large policies and with leaders.

I am still of the opinion—which I have repeatedly expressed both in speech and writing—that our program for change in the machinery of government is less well worked out than our program for economic change. It requires far more thought than it has been given. The rallying cry and the working program of a strong labor party in the next few years will be concerned far more with economic measures and the goal of the coöperative commonwealth than with the particular plan of a constitutional change, always provided that we insist on the fact that a mandate for economic change implies a mandate for sufficient political change to make it possible to carry out our program.

This brief discussion of the necessity for capturing political power brings us face to face with the most challenging of all our American failures. That is, our failure to organize any strong party which consciously represents the great masses of workers who look toward the coöperative commonwealth. The debates on philosophy and tactics carried on with so much bitterness by our working-class parties and sects leave the masses almost untouched. Neither their discontent nor their rising hopes have yet found expression in a mighty and militant party. The Roosevelt interlude has temporarily strengthened the opinion (an opinion not at all borne out by an examination of the facts), that it may be possible to use for our salvation one or the other of the two old parties or a strong leader or a group of leaders chosen indiscriminately out of both parties. In New York City the more progressive workers rushed to support LaGuardia, a nominal Republican. In California a veteran Socialist like Upton Sinclair actually persuaded himself that he could best advance Socialism by turning nominal Democrat and proceeding to try to carry out the following amazing program: (1) To win the Democratic gubernatorial nomination; (2) to win election as governor of California; and (3) in the space of one term, single-handed and irrespective of the rest of the country, to conquer poverty in California, principally by building up a new economic order through the colonization of some of the unemployed and the employment of the rest of them in factories to produce goods to exchange for food. So the author of innumerable Socialist books crowns his career by writing with sublime naïveté, *"How I, Governor of California, Abolished Poverty."*

This trust in a political messiah and this slowness to build up a large working-class party are made to order for the growth of Fascism. It is the theme of this book that the hope of successful resistance to Fascism is the hope of building a party with a philosophy and some such program as we have described. There is no time for Socialism in America to grow like a coral island. It is better to be right than to be President, but it is not much good being right unless once in a while you can elect a President! As contrasted with a type of all too gradual Socialism, it is exceedingly important that American Socialists should turn to what is usually regarded as the left in the vigor of their plan; but we have to make contacts with the great mass of workers, in country and city, in factory and office, who are to the right of us. In the nature of the thing the basis of any large party of the workers must be an insistence that it represents the interests of the workers, and in particular that it must immediately set about the process of socializing key industries. If we add to this a regard for the peace of the world and a fraternal sympathy for the struggle of the workers in other lands to be free, we shall have laid down a sufficient charter for a mass movement which Socialists can educate, with the mighty aid of its own inherent logic, into a rapidly growing acceptance of Socialism.

Of course, most Socialists feel that the logical thing would be for the masses to come into the Socialist Party. That party is not coextensive with the Socialist movement, but there would have been mighty little Socialism without it. Whatever our grievances against those who profess to be friends of our philosophy but who persist in remaining outside, however sincere our assurance of welcome to those who will come in, we should lose our supreme opportunity were we to turn away from a genuine mass movement because it did not precisely follow the lines dear to our heart. In other words, Socialists who appreciate the gravity of the crisis and who know how little time is to be lost, will be ready if their party does not itself become a mass party of the workers, to help in the creation of such a party. It is not an easy task. We do not want to emulate our friends of that little group called the Conference for Political Labor Action, who just the other day rechristened themselves with the resounding name, the American Workers Party. For Socialists or other radicals to call a convention and recapture themselves, gets nowhere and retards progress. We are ready to come into a mass movement, but we want to be sure that it is a mass movement. We must deal with individuals, not as individuals, but as spokesmen for various groups. These leaders and spokesmen may be rising young men and women. They need not be heads of existing unions and farm organizations; indeed, in the unlikely event that some of these gentlemen should espouse a new party, unless first they had themselves been converted, that party would be more likely to go off on a nationalist, small-scale-farmer-and-trade-union-capitalist tangent, than in a Socialist direction. Certainly the Socialist Party never again ought to go into a coalition like that of 1924, when we endorsed La-Follette for President and did more than our share to work for him at a time when most of our colleagues were fighting Socialist candidates for Congress in favor of Republicans and Democrats. In any new mass party we should preserve our identity at least for educational purposes as the Independent Labor Party once did within the British Labor Party, or as the Socialist League does now. Since the great issues are national, we should have to take precautions in affiliating with state farmer-labor parties which might dicker their souls away with the old parties in national elections.

I am not laying down an authoritative program for the Socialist Party. That is for a Socialist convention to do. I am not predicting the sure and speedy appearance of a farmer-labor party with Socialist aid, and certainly I do not believe that such a party can make satisfactory headway without Socialist aid. I am insisting that it is time for the Socialist Party and for Socialists and near-Socialists outside the party to subordinate all doctrinal and factional differences to a mighty effort to capture the imagination and successfully to organize the workers with hand and brain into a political party. It is time to stop talking about "holding the fort" when what we have to do is to capture the country. It is the time to realize that vital movements can and must grow quickly, that long before we can win the government by adding a few thousand members here, and electing a mayor there, and a congressman in another place, we shall have been swept, and our countrymen with us, into the disaster of Fascism or the catastrophe of war. It is not in our American scheme of things possible to develop the congressional bloc which can adequately represent the workers' interest. It is not the formation of a league which will endorse men, regardless of their party labels. The Anti-Saloon League may have got prohibition that way, but it did not keep it; and to get one specific thing like prohibition or women's suffrage is a very different thing from capturing power to establish the coöperative commonwealth. Names do mean something even if they are only Republican and Democrat. The interests which finance the old parties will be shaken loose from what they have owned so long with far more difficulty than a new party can be formed. The very complexity of our government requires a disciplined party to get anywhere. To build a genuine labor party is infinitely more desirable and ought not to be intrinsically more difficult than it was to build the Republican Party in the middle of the eighteen-fifties. This is the achievement which matters. It can be hastened by joining the Socialist Party now and working in it and through it for a mightier movement.

Let no reader say, because I have emphasized a political party, that I expect to see men and women vote in Utopia. The organization and maintenance of a party itself is more than a matter of voting. I have insisted ever since I became a Socialist that there must be economic organization of the workers on the industrial field, not alone for their immediate advantage and for their education in solidarity, but in order to add the weapon of economic power to supplement the power of the ballot. That the functions of a political party and of a labor union are so different that neither ought to dominate the other from without, does not mean that unions can do their duty to workers and ignore independent working-class political action, or that Socialists can be indifferent to the organization and conduct of unions. It is old and sound Socialist doctrine that a triumphant labor movement must organize industrially in unions, politically in a party, and as consumers—so far as lost opportunities will permit—in consumers' coöperatives. This threefold organization needs to be supplemented in America, perhaps more than in any country in the world, if we hope for success, by the sympathetic support of engineers, and by the mass support of organized farmers. Socialists cannot too strongly deny the charge that we intend to drive the farmers off their farms. Rather we want to make their occupation of them more secure and more remunerative. Nevertheless, the basis of any but the most temporary coalition between farmers and wage. or salary workers must be a dawning recognition by farmers that they are workers and that they should be rewarded as workers and not as small capitalists or business men. There is no logical impossibility that we can help farmers to see that the fulfillment of the best American tradition is in the establishment of the coöperative commonwealth and not in various populist nostrums.

This brief discussion of the action necessary if we are to move toward the coöperative commonwealth, would be hopelessly incomplete were we to fail once more to emphasize that the world which machinery has made so small has become the unit of organization for man's happiness and freedom. No practical program of Socialism or social progress in America can be drawn by men who will not understand and accept the power of national sentiment and of the state organized on national lines. But to accept this as a present fact is not to accept it as a cause for rejoicing, much less as the ultimate and final word on social organization. Today the best service that America can render the world is to fulfill her own most glorious traditions and to rescue herself from the death grip of a disintegrating capitalism. This must be done, and can only be done, in allegiance to that program of peace which we have outlined in a previous chapter. While we are doing it we must steadily be laying the basis in education, and so far as possible in practical action, for that world organization under which alone can our immense natural resources and all the various skills of men in their management be coördinated in the final conquest of poverty, and the rivalry of nations become emulation in the arts and sciences.

So we come to the end of our book but not of our struggle. By no miracle can the next generation be as well off as the last, and that, God knows, was bad enough. We shall either be much worse off or much better. We shall have made our choice perhaps without knowing its fateful quality. We shall rush headlong into the devastation of new world war and the long agonies of recovery, or we shall have played with the passions, the prejudices, the stupidities and brutalities of Fascism as a prelude to cataclysmic destruction. Or we shall set our hearts and our hopes upon the coöperative commonwealth. We shall use the brains which have given us such marvelous powers of invention to control the things we have made and to use them to bring forth abundance. And in sharing that abundance we and our children after us shall celebrate the end of the long night of exploitation, poverty and war, and the dawn of a day of beauty and peace, freedom and fellowship.

INDEX

Abundance, 6; destruction of, as way to prosperity, 7; era of increasing, 18; remuneration in a world of, 221.

Acreage, reduction of, 99-100.

Aggressor nation, lack of means to define, 179.

Agricultural Adjustment Act, an indictment of society, 7; and farm prices, 91; analysis of, 98-101; and N.R.A., 105.

Agriculture, subsidy to, 90.

America, its respite from fate, 10; economic individualism in, 17-18; great fortunes in, 20-21. *See also* United States, Latin America.

American Federation of Labor, Gen. Johnson's declaration to, 124; under N.R.A., 131-133; changes necessary to make it vital force, 133-141.

Anti-War Congress, 155, 156.

Arizona, record Socialist vote in, 142.

Armament, expenditures on, 3. *See also* Munitions.

Armistice (1918), joy at, 1.

Army, enlarged expenditure on, 126; Administration eulogy of, 126n. *See also* Red Army.

Assembly, liberty of, 37.

Austria, nationalism in, 64.

Autarchy, 5, 14, 126.

Ayres, Leonard, depression chart of, 22.

Balkan states, terror in, 37, 53.

Bank credit, stimulation of, 95, 116, 117; control of, 121.

Bank deposits, federal guarantee of 89.

Bankers, discredited, 86, 88, 128.

Banking system, epidemic failures in, 85, 87; patched up by Roosevelt, 88-90; how it might have been nationalized, 208-209.

Beals, Carleton, on totalitarian state, 49.

Bill of Rights, American, 36.

Black Shirts, Italian, 37, 57, 193.

Bolivia, undeclared war with Paraguay, 3.

Bonds, foreign, 5. *See also* Securities.

Books, Hitler's bonfire of, 10.

Boycott, of Germany, 68; by farmers, 86; war danger in, 167.

Bridgeport, Conn., Socialist victory in, 142.

British Labor Party, 64; declarations against war, 69, 168, 181.

Browder, Earl, on united front, 152.

Brown Shirts, German, 37.

Buck, Pearl, 6.

Budget, national, 95; Roosevelt's message on, 113.

Bulgaria, terror in, 37.